THE CONNECTION CURRICULUM

THE CONNECTION CURRICULUM

Igniting Positive Change in Schools
Through Sustainable Connection

MATT PITMAN

Praise for *The Connection Curriculum*

Connection is indeed what we all need, but it can also be problematic because there are so many different things to connect to and different ways to be connected. Matt has written a book with a strong message full of content that is very honest and practical.

Dr Yong Zhao, PhD – foundation distinguished professor, author

Matt is an enthusiast for finding better outcomes for more learners through deep connection in education. This infectious energy finds its way onto every page of this thought-provoking book.

Dr Phil Cummins – associate professor, co-host of the *Game Changers* podcast

Matt's book gives us the luxury of pondering and considering one of the human sides of education; a side that we all know makes a difference but hesitate to dig into. It helps us to understand just how to build deep and ongoing connection in learning spaces, playgrounds, meetings and surrounding community. This book is worth reading, discussing and implementing with a team of your favourite educators.

Pip Cleaves, principal

Through detailed practical insights connected strongly to the academic literature, Matt provides a welcome roadmap for both teachers and school leaders to consider how best to build sustainable, whole-school connections beyond short-term efforts. It is a fantastic resource for school leadership teams interested in planning for and developing their school's growth in whole-school connectedness.

Christopher Hudson – author, leader, academic

Schools must be connected, they are integral parts of our communities. Building connections and connected communities has never been more important than it is now. This book is an essential read for all teachers and school leaders.

Mathew Green – school leader, host of *The Art of Teaching* podcast

This book is essential for every teacher, leader or administrator aiming to foster better student-teacher-community relationships, reverse disengagement and ultimately improve the vibe of school communities and student outcomes.

James Vella – school leader

Published in 2024 by Amba Press, Melbourne, Australia
www.ambapress.com.au

© Matthew Pitman 2024

All rights reserved. No part of this book may be reproduced or transmitted in any form or by any means, electronic or mechanical, including photocopying, recording or by any information storage and retrieval system, without prior permission in writing from the publisher.

Cover design: Tess McCabe
Internal design: Amba Press
Editor: Rica Dearman

ISBN: 9781923116535 (pbk)
ISBN: 9781923116542 (ebk)

A catalogue record for this book is available from the National Library of Australia.

Contents

Acknowledgements	ix
About the author	xi
Introduction	1

Part 1: Understanding connection — 11

Chapter 1	The connection journey	13
Chapter 2	Non-negotiables	35
Chapter 3	The Connection Curriculum framework	51

Part 2: Building connection — 61

Alignment — 63

Chapter 4	Know thyself *Focus Area 1: Identity*	65
Chapter 5	What am I doing? *Focus Area 2: Purpose*	79

Adaptability — 93

Chapter 6	Opportunity creators > Problem-solvers *Focus Area 3: Creativity*	95
Chapter 7	Right in the feels! *Focus Area 4: Empathic curiosity*	109

Autonomy — 123

Chapter 8	A seat at the table, not just a sausage in bread *Focus Area 5: Voice*	125
Chapter 9	Houston, we have lift-off! *Focus Area 6: Permission*	139

Part 3: Sustaining connection　153
　　Chapter 10　Making it all work　155

Conclusion　169
References　175

Acknowledgements

A year ago, I had no idea I had a book idea swimming around in my brain, let alone that I had the ability to put it all down on paper. Writing a book is a difficult thing; it is time-consuming, frustrating, confidence building and just as often confidence destroying.

This continuum of emotions, imposter syndrome, challenges and triumphs has only been possible with the support of my wife, Marina. You, along with our daughter, Olivia, have been unwavering pillars of support throughout this lengthy process, and this book would not have been completed without you both. The support and sacrifice of time and space was invaluable, and the reason this book exists is because of your commitment to holding my hand along this journey. Thank you, I love you.

Additionally, a number of friends and colleagues read different versions of this book as it came together, and each perspective elevated the quality of the content within exponentially. Without your honest feedback and the sacrifice of your personal time, particularly during holiday breaks, it would not have come this far. Dr Yong Zhao, Dr Phil Cummins, Pip Cleaves, Christopher Hudson, James Vella, Mathew Green and Kate Pizzey, I cannot thank you all enough!

About the author

Matt Pitman is a school leader, teacher, husband and father. He is obsessed with learning and has been fuelling a passion for connection and studying its associated research for years. From pastoral care programs, student voice and agency initiatives, and exploration of student transition from primary to secondary school, he has analysed connection from multiple angles, and that knowledge has culminated in this book and the components of The Connection Curriculum.

Matt began his education career in Catholic Education, gaining extensive experience in the leadership of curriculum teams and programs, before switching to focus on student wellbeing, student improvement and community engagement. In Government schools he has led Positive Education and student support programs working with students, parents and staff to develop new understandings of the needs of young people in the 21st century.

Matt is currently part of a dynamic Edventurous leadership team designing a new model for schooling in the picturesque Macedon Ranges, Victoria; a model that is bound by play, exploration and connection. He is driven by his passion for change and his personal 'why': *to empower people with creativity and curiosity so that we can all create positive change in our world.*

Introduction

Playing it safe is hurting our students

I want to start this book with a bold statement: *schools need to get their act together regarding connection.* Connectedness in schools is widely misunderstood in terms of what it looks like (García-Moya, 2020; Gümüş et al., 2022; Kim et al., 2023; Rose et al., 2022), and how it plays into the primary focus of many of these schools: academic achievement.

When I consider academic achievement and how it is measured and compared, I'm thinking grades, regardless of whether they are represented as letters, numbers, percentages and ranks. For far too long, schools have focused on this type of data while superficially addressing many of the foundational factors responsible for creating "good grades" (Allen et al., 2018; Burns & Frangiosa, 2021; Hardy, 2015; Schneider, 2017), such as connection.

> The Centers for Disease Control and Prevention (2023) defines school connectedness as a "students' belief that peers and adults in the school support, value, and care about their individual well-being as well as their academic progress" (para. 1).
>
> Students who feel more connected to school are *"less* likely to engage in risky behaviours" and *"more* likely to engage in positive health behaviours" (para. 2).

Contemporary schools have nailed the language in their public-facing materials (social media, websites, marketing materials and enrolment packages), and savvy leaders have perfected the art of the parent information night plug. Generally, schools aim for perfection of results rather than empowerment of people (Schneider, 2017) – this is despite the knowledge, skills and desire to change from this established status quo.

A cursory internet search will uncover countless blog posts, podcasts and articles begging for a change to the systems, processes and methods we run our schools by, yet we still find ourselves in a similar position, year after year.

The most bizarre part of it all is we have managed (for the most part) to make our way out of a global pandemic which absolutely changed the way we live, communicate and connect (Qvortrup & Lykkegaard, 2024; Tomkunas et al., 2023). Schools soldiered on through this pandemic and had the opportunity to create some of the most innovative means for delivering learning, extracurricular activities and human connectedness (Sahlberg, 2020; Tomkunas et al., 2023).

Now, as we sit on the other side, COVID-19 may as well be Voldemort (from the Harry Potter novels for the uninitiated) – we do not speak its name and we pretend it did not happen. The COVID-19 pandemic was horrible, and I do not blame anyone for swiftly moving on for the sake of their health and wellbeing, but the lessons we learned about what works and what does not should have remained (Qvortrup & Lykkegaard, 2024; Sahlberg, 2020).

As I write this introduction, I am concerned about too much pandemic talk; I do not want this book to be latched to a specific point in time as the message and the tools in this book should be timeless, but the events of the past few years are a tribute to the unrelenting rigidity of our educational system (Sahlberg, 2020). Schools discarding the lessons learned and returning to pre-COVID practices highlights this.

We had the catalyst and the platforms to create change. We saw incredibly powerful models of instruction brought to life, including game-changing innovations in pedagogy, wellbeing and communication (Qvortrup & Lykkegaard, 2024), but when the bells rang out and the school gates reopened, so did the old ways of running a school.

Some questions worth asking are:

1. Were schools connected *pre-pandemic*?
2. Have we really reconnected *post-pandemic*?

My memory can be a little bit foggy at the best of times, but I do not remember living in a time of educational utopia pre-2020. So, why have we returned to this state of being? Research suggests (as do collegial discussions through professional networks) that school refusal is increasing across the country (see Figure 1 opposite) and the globe (Fray et al., 2023a; McDonald et al., 2023; Walters, 2023; Yan, 2023).

Figure 1: Student attendance level for Years 1–10 students in all schools in Australia, time series

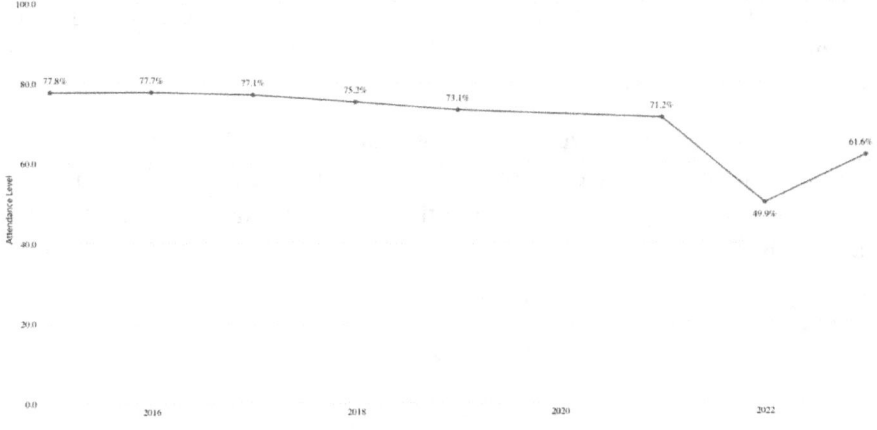

(AUSTRALIAN CURRICULUM, ASSESSMENT AND REPORTING AUTHORITY (ACARA), 2023)

Staff, despite strong relationships with those in their school communities, are leaving (see Table 1 below) what they once may have referred to as their 'calling' and their passion (Craig et al., 2023; Fray et al., 2023b). Principals and school leaders are under fire from parents who are lost and searching for answers (Fotheringham et al., 2022; Wang et al., 2023). We are looking at the tip of the iceberg while the base hidden deep under the water is slowly sinking us.

Table 1: Proportion intending to leave before retirement over time by workforce segments

Workforce segment	2019	2020	2021	2022
Teacher workforce	26%	21%	26%	35%
Classroom teachers	28%	23%	28%	34%
Middle leaders	26%	21%	26%	35%
Senior leaders	19%	16%	20%	30%
Casual/relief teachers	23%	18%	22%	28%

(AUSTRALIAN INSTITUTE FOR TEACHING AND SCHOOL LEADERSHIP (AITSL), 2023)

Therefore, we have a connection crisis. We are focusing on money, resources and filling teaching positions, but not on the people benefitting from that funding, the future impact of those resources and the humans behind our workforce of passionate and highly skilled teachers. We were coasting pre-pandemic, then we scrambled during it, and now we are in a state of deficit. We have all let it go this far as a profession.

As an education system, we should have continued to innovate on a larger scale, and we should have continued to be curious. But, for the most part, it feels as though we did not. The entire system returned to comfortable, predictable and safe.

Unfortunately, *safe is hurting our students.*

What is this?

Connection is an essential part of developing the whole person (Okabe-Miyamoto et al., 2021; Pandya & Lodha, 2021; Van Orden et al., 2021) – the same whole person almost every single school website opens talking about. When connection is lacking, there is a bifurcation of that whole person (Van Orden et al., 2021), the staff member, the student. We desperately need to genuinely focus on connection, on play and on culture, and stop using them as tools of marketing and propaganda.

Our need to connect and the skills required to build and maintain those connections has been developed over thousands of years. Our ability to connect is an essential component of the earliest stages of the lifespan (Holt-Lunstad, 2022; Pandya & Lodha, 2021; Van Orden et al., 2021), and in those stages, connection is fostered or stunted, particularly during childhood, as at its core, connection is a survival skill, a coping strategy and a lifeline (Holt-Lunstad, 2022).

This book, *The Connection Curriculum*, exists because the research is clear: if schools do not shift their focus to sustainably building and supporting the maintenance of whole-school connectedness, they are doing immeasurable damage to their communities (Allen, 2020; Arslan, 2021; Korpershoek et al., 2020), and robbing every single person within of their chance to be whole.

As a leader and a teacher, I can see the growing disconnection. The lack of targeted and sustainable work surrounding whole-school connectedness being undertaken in practice – despite the constantly growing field of research that could be supporting its implementation (Allen, 2020; Arslan,

2021; García-Moya, 2020; Kim et al., 2023; Korpershoek et al., 2020; Rose et al., 2022) – is concerning for me and many within our profession. I do want to be clear about that last statement. I am focusing on sustainable and whole-school connection, not short-term efforts or personal connections in individual classrooms. While these are important, I want you to think bigger than your own classes.

This book provides a simple guide to addressing common areas that need some additional time, effort and resources to create the environment necessary for connection to flourish and be maintained over time. The Connection Curriculum is not a traditional curriculum map documenting what is to be taught and learned, so much as a description of the conditions in which real and better learning might take place in your context.

At its core, it is a set of principles of practice that can operate individually, collectively and systemically. These tools are the distillation of my scholarly reading, presented here as a toolkit for unlocking the potential to effect positive change in schools. It is a toolkit that you can adopt to help your community create a dynamic of constructive connection.

This book does not exist to tell you that your school or your community is doing everything wrong. In fact, my intention is quite the opposite. In writing this book, I want to help you to realise the work you are already undertaking, so you can celebrate and champion the amazing people and efforts your community is already engaged with. But I also want to encourage you to think more consistently and to go much further with your thinking, planning and facilitating, so that you can take the foundations you have and build a sustainable model, purpose-built for your community.

This book is an exercise in highlighting the now and planning for growth in the future. Both aspects cannot be addressed specifically within one book, so unfortunately, this is not going to do the work for you. This book is designed to give you the markers, but you fill the contextual information. You take these must-haves and make them fit until they become *definitely haves*. You know your school, your staff and your families, and I am not writing this book to tell you how to connect with your school community specifically.

No two schools or workplaces are the same, I do not know you personally or your specific context and the nuances that make up your school community. I am writing this to tell you what you need to focus on when you are working with your people towards building stronger connection.

As Simon Sinek (2019) would say, it is an infinite game and we have been predominantly playing with a finite mindset. We will discuss constant reflection shortly, but in my mind an approach to sustainable connection is one that never reaches an end point.

You may argue that when a student graduates, you could collect some data and find out how connected they felt. They are moving on, after all, that seems finite. But you need to be focused on the whole school, not the individuals. Just because a graduate felt connected on some level to their school after six years does not mean a new student in Year 7, despite having three siblings attend in the past, feels the same way. Connection is *ongoing*.

You are not trying to connect one student at a time and for the period they attend. You are trying to create an environment that grabs every student that walks through your gate for eternity. They should leave feeling like they could always come back. Create a safe place for them and they just might. I am aiming for the big lofty goals here and so should you. The benefits of creating this level of change, as we will discuss throughout the book, are well worth the effort.

Depending on your context, that change may be small, or it may be significant. Either way, the change is necessary and, no matter which way you look at it, change does not happen in a vacuum, change does not occur without resistance (Ford et al., 2021; Fullan, 2015). Throughout this book, I will be asking you, as the reader, as the representative for your community, to really consider what work needs to be done in your very specific space.

The questions I will encourage you to ask might be confronting depending on the nature of your current circumstances and, let us face it, often when something needs to be done, that requires effort, resources and a long time frame, people will naturally resist (Fullan, 2015). The way I see it, if there is no resistance or discourse, if the journey does not fill my stomach with butterflies, then it is not the right way to move forward, and I am on the wrong track.

If this book stirs up a bit of a hornet's nest, I will be looking at that as the first in a long line of challenges to meet. If it is upsetting, it means the initial message has sunk in just past the surface. It means it may hold some truth. That is a good start. That means we can get on with fixing it.

Who is this for?

It has always surprised me how many different genres of books educators will read to broaden their understanding of their profession, such as philosophy, business and self-care, but how few outside of education will read books on teaching, learning and schools. This book is clearly aimed, and no doubt marketed, towards teachers, support staff and leaders in schools. That is my context and therefore the lens through which my knowledge and experience is presented, however, I would hope that the lessons here and the six Focus Areas of The Connection Curriculum would be beneficial to a whole host of organisations, businesses and individuals.

Learning about the history of Apple, Microsoft or Patagonia did not perfectly apply to my contextual practice as a teacher in a school, but it did fuel my curiosity and widen my knowledge on people, purpose, passion and productivity. I am a more effective teacher because of this broad perspective, and I hope that school staff feel as though the content in this book speaks to you specifically, but more widely, that the lessons on connection are universal.

Change requires leadership, but this book is not aimed specifically at existing leaders. Everyone who works in a school must be a leader of change when it comes to connection. The emphasis here is on you as a teacher, but not purely on your work in the classroom. Through the messages and tools in this book, your role shifts towards creating influence and momentum with all of those around you. The messages in this book will help you to emphasise a community movement that requires great leadership, but that leadership can be in the form of teachers, students and parents. Every single member of your community can demonstrate the leadership required to create momentum towards connection, with your support.

If you read this book and feel as though it may benefit someone you know, I would really appreciate you passing the details on as well as any feedback or information regarding its implementation in your context. This book is for anyone looking to address the tangled knot that is managing, leading and belonging to a community in our contemporary, digital, globalised world.

If we can understand the people around us and how each one of us is connected to the whole, we can start to untangle the knot, unlearn the old ways and build sustainable, connected communities.

What is to come?

This book is split into three parts.

- **Part 1: Understanding connection** aims to address the question *what is connection?* Chapter 1 unpacks the literature to identify the nature of what I am calling the connection journey; a series of Landmarks essential to foster a true sense of connection within an individual and their community. Chapter 2 puts a spotlight on the non-negotiables when considering change towards sustainable connection, setting the scene for a genuine attempt at organisational change in this space. Chapter 3 introduces The Connection Curriculum framework, its rationale, its aims and how it maps to the Landmarks of the connection journey.
- **Part 2: Building connection** aims to address the question *what do I need to develop and maintain sustainable connection?* Chapters 4 through to 9 take a deep dive, unpacking each of the six Focus Areas of The Connection Curriculum one by one and in detail, providing you with the inspiration and guidelines to start your school, organisation or community on the track to being truly connected.
- **Part 3: Sustaining connection** aims to address the question *where do we go from here?* Chapter 10 is the final chapter, bringing The Connection Curriculum together and providing you with not only a summary, but some last ideas, thoughts and, if need be, arguments to assist with starting genuine movement on the connection journey in your context.

I hope the book proves useful and, at the very least, an enjoyable read.

Figure 2: The Connection Curriculum

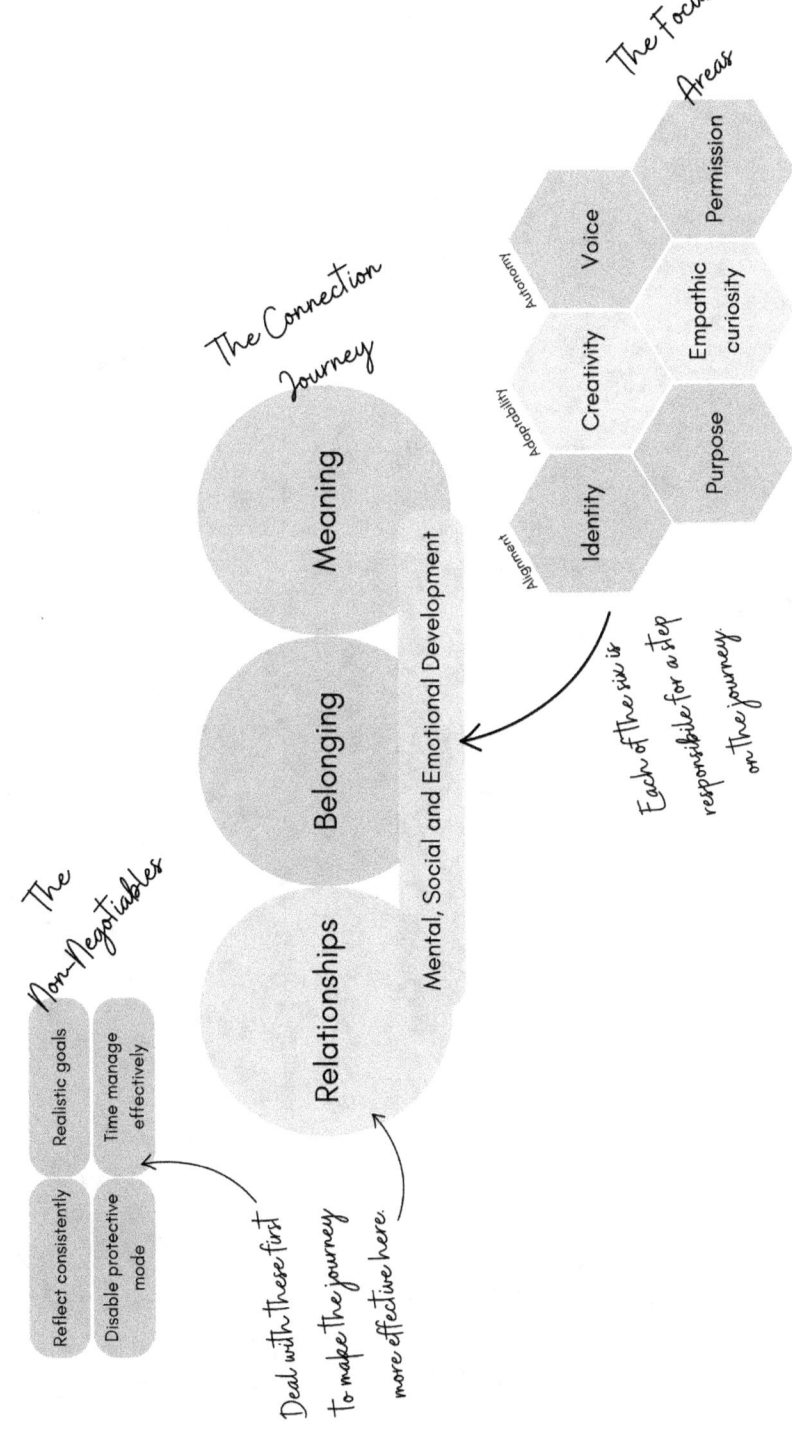

Introduction 9

PART I
UNDERSTANDING CONNECTION

"We are like islands in the sea, separate on the surface but connected in the deep"

WILLIAM JAMES

The hardest part of any change is the start.

Habits are hard to break especially when they are established in years of practice and indoctrinated into those who join the cause. To address connection, we need to rethink and re-establish a clear understanding of what connectivity is and how we approach a change towards sustainable, whole-school connection. Adam Grant (2021), author of *Think Again: The Power of Knowing What You Don't Know*, posits: "Rethinking needs to become a regular habit. Unfortunately, traditional methods of education don't always *allow* students to form that habit."

Part 1: Understanding connection aims to break the habits limiting our capacity to be connected by starting the processes of rethinking connection and asking a simple question: *What is it?*

To address this question, a review of connection literature is featured in Chapter 1 with three specific intentions: to redefine the key components of connection as a concept; to identify a new benchmark for connectivity; and to understand the components of the connection journey. Chapter 2 addresses common barriers and reframes these as non-negotiables. We cannot attempt to start until we accept these factors as: 1) existing, and 2) part of the experience. Chapter 3 introduces The Connection Curriculum framework, its dimensions and Focus Areas, setting the scene for your collective journey of connection.

CHAPTER I
The connection journey

There is a fantastic array of research linked to connection out there in the world. The field specific to schools and education is large enough in itself, but more widely, connection is defined, discussed, deciphered and decoded for its use in business, medicine, psychology and politics. To read, note, highlight and persist through this huge amount of research is a task beyond the resources of the already busy teacher, parent or student, let alone bringing everything back into our own contexts in education.

This chapter aims to do the heavy lifting for you firstly by addressing the confusion and misunderstandings surrounding connection as a concept and introducing one of the core concepts of the book: the connection journey. Secondly, each of the three Landmarks of the connection journey are introduced and detailed, along with a discussion of mental, social and emotional development. Finally, the chapter concludes by discussing the nature of the journey and the importance of taking the first steps towards a sustainably connected community.

Understanding the journey

It is my belief that everything that makes an organisation successful stems from connection. Connection to an ideal, a belief, a purpose, even a person, is one of the most powerful drivers behind change, growth and success (Gümüş et al., 2022). If you were to suggest that any system, organisation or community could operate successfully and sustainably without a sense of connection, sense of belonging or meaning, I would prepare myself eagerly for a friendly debate.

> In a meta-analysis of 51 studies on school connection (the authors used the term 'belonging'), Allen et al. (2018) concluded connection within a school community:
> - Positively correlates to higher academic performance;
> - Reduces rates of absence and increases rates of school completion;
> - Lowers truancy and improves behaviour, engagement and self-efficacy;
> - Contributes to high levels of happiness, self-esteem and positive identity; and
> - Reduces occurrences of violence, bullying, vandalism and risk-taking behaviours.

Establishing high levels of connectivity between members and their community, therefore, is concomitant with improved wellbeing, positivity and meaning (Arslan, 2019; Šeboková et al., 2018). This is especially pertinent based on a study conducted by Virtanen et al. (2019), highlighting a systematic reduction in wellbeing across adolescents post-primary school, and one by Arslan (2019) concluding, where a student's and a school's values are aligned, peer groups are more likely to create a shared identity that fosters a sense of shared belonging that is driven by social values, rather than academic ones.

Connecting parents to their child's education allows for caregivers to be active contributors to their learning, understand and empathise with their performance, and effectively support young people to plan for their futures (Allen et al., 2023; El Zaatari & Ibrahim, 2021). Uslu and Gizir (2017) found that where parental involvement is encouraged, student motivation increased, along with improvements in effort and work ethic, and resilience to challenges.

Connection in the staffroom is intrinsically linked to a sense of wellbeing, feelings of worth and value, and motivation within the profession, with Skaalvik and Skaalvik (2021) stating that shared values correlated positively with career satisfaction and teacher retention. As the reality of education across the globe becomes more and more reliant on collaboration, a connected staff are more likely to work together inside and outside of the classroom, sharing experiences and successes as a collective, reframing the profession from any notions of individuality and towards supportive partnerships (Allen et al., 2023; Skaalvik & Skaalvik, 2021).

Therefore, across all aspects of a school environment, connection is one of the most important components of what makes a school successful, its students thrive and its community flourish. Yet, a significant portion of the literature suggests it is also one of the most mistreated, mismanaged and mishandled (García-Moya, 2020; Kim et al., 2023; Rose et al., 2022). The core reason behind this is our own misunderstanding of what it means to be connected to something or someone (Gümüş et al., 2022). Connection is not an event that then solidifies a bond and is infinitely retained. Connection is a continuous *journey*.

Connection is one of the first things we understand as important when we are born, and one of the last things we hold on to before we die. It is hidden and invisible, but inherently part of our DNA and essential to the human experience (Gümüş et al., 2022). What it means to connect has changed over time, and we certainly discuss being more connected than ever before, especially via digital means. But true, deep and sustainable connection requires several interconnected components, both to meet the standards outlined in the literature and those that form the foundation for everything forthcoming in this book.

There are three key Landmarks on the connection journey, each prominent and interconnected in the research, but not as often in practice. The Landmarks are:

- Relationships;
- Belonging; and
- Meaning.

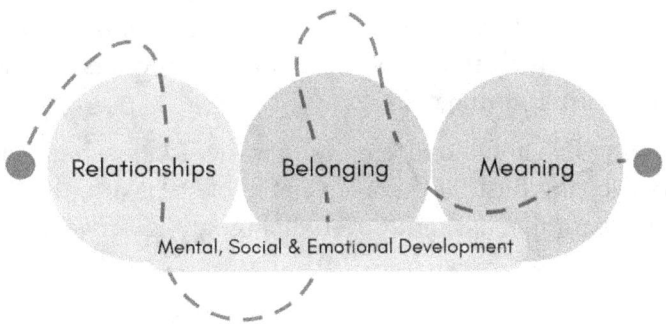

Throughout the connection journey is also an additional factor: *mental, social and emotional development*. While not a Landmark on the journey, mental, social and emotional development is a determinant of health and wellbeing, and an essential component in the development of the whole person (Stirling & Emery, 2016). Mental, social and emotional development will have significant influence on the success of the connection journey and vice versa, depending on your specific context, particularly the age of the students or individuals in your community. More on this shortly.

When relationships, belonging and meaning are a focus in schools, the developmental potential of a young person is increased (Long & Guo, 2023). The three Landmarks are both agonist and antagonist on the connection journey, both relying on and relied upon for the development of each of the other two for true, deep connection. The more common reality, however, is that they are rarely linked together; even when successfully implemented, they are often siloed from each other, diminishing their potential impact (Zhang et al., 2018).

It would be incredibly shocking if your school or organisation did not address one, two or all three of these pieces, but if they are isolated from each other, you are building each component but not the greater whole.

In many schools, relationships are a core focus at the heart of the values and mission (Arslan, 2019). Belonging is attributed to events, awards or extracurricular programs, such as performing arts or sports. Meaning is driven by conversations about learning, the future, subject selection and careers. None of these are wrong or damaging, but they form individual pieces, rather than feeding the whole-school connection journey.

Predominantly, schools focus on relationships, and so they should. John Hattie (2023), author of *Visible Learning: The Sequel: A Synthesis of Over 2,100 Meta-Analyses Relating to Achievement*, identified student-teacher relationships to have an effect size of .47 (see Figure 3 opposite). (Anything above .4 indicates high significance.) And this is a good thing; however, *connection is greater than relationships, it is more than relationships*. After poring through the research, I understand the limitations of relationships masquerading as real connection.

I am not writing this book to discredit the work of thousands of incredible researchers over the past 50 years. Yes, relationships are pivotal and can be long-lasting, impactful and overwhelmingly positive for students, but relationships can also be ingenuine, surface level, functional and controlling. They also cannot be where your connection journey begins and ends.

Figure 3: Ten selected effect sizes: what works best for learning in schools? (Hattie, 2023)

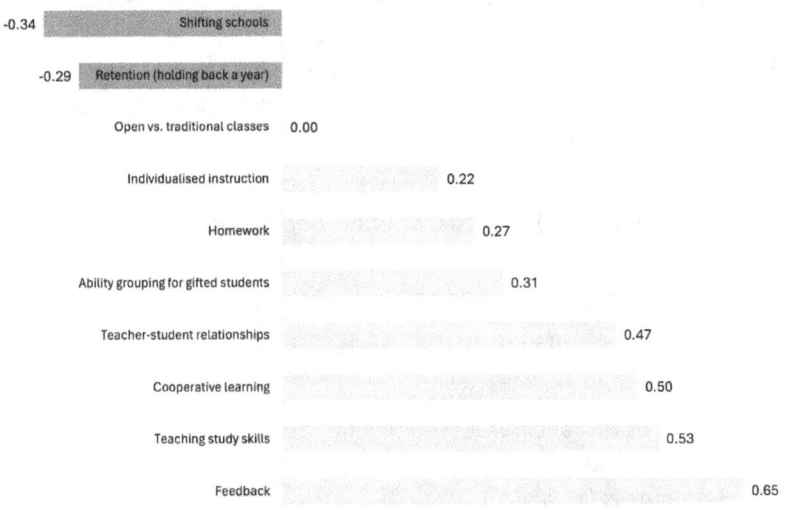

The following sections detail the rationale and provocations for each of the three Landmarks on the connection journey, setting the stage for your own engagement with connection and community-wide positive change discussed later in the book. The final section will discuss the influence of development and the cyclical, non-linear and sometimes random route connection can take – especially with young people.

Landmark 1: Relationships

Before starting off on this journey, I want to be very clear: relationships are essential. No school, business or organisation can possibly underestimate the power that relationships hold, both to build and destroy them (Gregory & Mebane, 2020). After the introduction and short preamble to this chapter, this may seem like a quick backpedal, but I never said they were not important, just that relationships do not equate to connection. You can have a relationship with someone but not feel connected to them; however, you cannot feel connected to someone without an existing relationship.

Relationships are in fact vital to the foundation of everything this book represents. They are the starting point on the connection journey. If you think about it, this really should not be a surprise. Every journey starts with a relationship. Even a solo trip around the world is about reconciling with oneself; is this not a relationship? The journey to true connection always starts with relationships. No matter the time, place or context. If you are working with people, you must start with building a relationship.

> Van Bergen, Graham and Sweller (2020) conducted a series of interviews with 96 students from Grades 3–10 to hear their memories of former teachers to determine the quality and consistency of these relationships over time. Three groups were formed:
> - Two containing students with disruptive behaviour (one in an alternative school, one in mainstream); and
> - One with no disruptive behaviour (in mainstream).
>
> Of the students who could recall a good relationship with a teacher, they were asked what made it this way.
> - 76 per cent of students discussed teacher behaviours directly:
>   - Kindness and care (38 per cent);
>   - Helpfulness (16 per cent);
>   - Humour (12 per cent); and
>   - Effective teaching (10 per cent).
> - 33 per cent of students in the disruptive-alternative school group could not recall any positive relationships with a teacher in the past.

Romantic, familial, professional or obligatory, the successful formation of a relationship will govern the level and quality of connections you can make and the longevity and impact of those connections (Sethi & Scales, 2020). In a school environment, this involves the careful deciphering of many cultural and societal nuances, but perhaps this is the same everywhere.

In any case, it is important to note that just like assuming connection, assuming you have a relationship with another person is a recipe for disaster. The connection journey is one that cannot operate on assumptions.

Consider this example... You, a teacher, return after a holiday break and a successful year. You are in the fortunate position of following your previous classes up into their next year level, a perfect result after such strong relationship building. You walk into your first class beaming; 60 minutes later, you leave dismayed. Nothing that you remembered to work last year was a success and the students seemed like completely different people. You have no idea what went wrong.

People are constantly changing. When we are drawn apart – even for the space of a few weeks over a school break – that could certainly be enough to warrant some additional groundwork. When the break is longer or the distance greater, you may need to start the foundational work all over again.

Relationships are incredibly complex. Young people are incredibly complex. This makes schools challenging, and potentially explosive environments for relationship building. In the example above, it is important that we understand the diminishing nature of relationships in a professional environment (Tataw, 2023). Friends and family can go weeks, months, years without substantial contact, but in a professional environment, this is simply not the case.

On return from a break, there may be threads that exist that make it easier to rekindle relationships, but without care, those threads cannot be woven into a previous form, or further into a strong and sustainable connection.

The fact is people change. Young people change often, sometimes daily. A two-week or eight-week break is substantial in the scheme of a young person's life. Assuming your previous relationship still exists or that you are the same people you were before the break, is to misunderstand and set yourself up for failure.

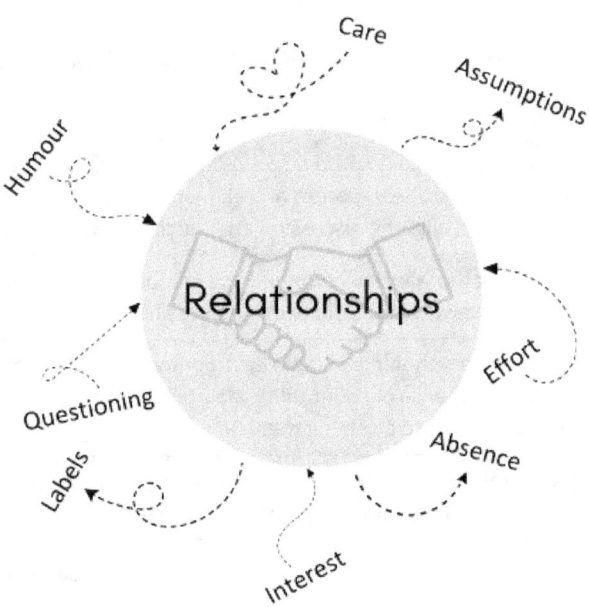

This is one of the reasons efforts to build real, long-lasting connection in schools fails. We pick up where we may have left off rather than starting the journey again. When we do this, we are treating professional relationships like familial relationships and fundamentally misunderstanding the nature of human interaction (Tataw, 2023).

Having a good relationship is not sufficient if the goal is connection. I have had many colleagues use the old teacher adage "they will work for you, if you get to know them". This is great if the aim is to develop a relationship for peace and harmony in the class, homework submitted on time or increasing average assessment scores. But these are all external to the young people in front of us.

When that student leaves that class, what then? What if they only have a strong relationship with one teacher or none? What if that teacher leaves the school? That one relationship becomes a dependency and one that could impact perception and the rest of the school experience (Stoll, 2020).

Now, we need to ask, is this the fault of the individual teacher, who strived to get to know their students and provide a personal and human approach to their practice? Certainly not. But imagine a whole-school approach to professional relationships rather than the random dispersal across a school. I think we can agree this would provide a safeguard against this phenomenon.

This takes work, of course. Below, in Table 2, you will find some strategies for developing community relationships.

Table 2: Strategies for cultivating positive relationships

Strategy	Description
Know your people	Knowing a student, parent or staff member's name and interests can assist with aligning discussion and outcomes with a supportive tone.
Give meaningful feedback	Noticing the way you communicate feedback or constructive concern can assist with overcoming challenges and conveys a growth mindset.
Create a positive environment	Create a psychologically safe environment by actively listening and creating a sense of community. Maintain high expectations and provide steps to attaining them.
Be respectful and sensitive	Value all community members' opinions and interests, and frame all actions and decisions towards reflection and learning.

(ADAPTED FROM RIMM-KAUFMAN & SANDILOS, 2015)

Landmark 2: Belonging

High levels of school connectedness are strongly linked to developing student motivation, engagement and improving academic results (Heinsch et al., 2020). This is something for all schools to strive towards, but beyond relationships, what does connection need to thrive and survive the tumultuous and dynamic reality of life?

Young people make decisions and choices which are primarily informed by their emotions. This can be problematic for schools as the human brain has many distinct centres, one responsible for emotions, and one responsible for language (Manwani & Gupta, 2020) and, unfortunately, they often do not work very well together.

Think back to a time when you were angry. Incredible Hulk-level angry. Could you describe in words why? Or are you more likely to yell, scream or physically throw your hands around in a fit? Emotions are incredibly hard to put into words because the brain is not wired to allow this to happen with ease. Think about the feeling of love. If you know it, you can certainly feel it, but can you put it easily into words?

Young people operate almost exclusively in a space in which they are physically unable to accurately describe how they feel, but that does not limit the importance of having the feelings themselves. Landmark 2 on the connection journey is belonging, or the feeling of being safe, accepted and a part of something larger than the self (Long & Guo, 2023).

Up until they graduate, young people spend a significant amount of their life in schools and, therefore, they must play a significant role in creating and maintaining social, emotional and academic pathways (Carney et al., 2017). When students feel they are cared for and part of a greater community, they are more likely to seek out opportunities to learn and exhibit fewer undesirable behaviours (Zeinalipour, 2022).

To make this desired state a reality, we need to make students feel they are part of the school, not just simply attendees or visitors. In primary school, students are looking to feel comfortable away from home after leaving their parents or carers. They are looking for safety, encouragement and the opportunity to make new friends (Bouchard & Berg, 2017). While students may enjoy their learning, at its core, it is not the subjects or the content necessarily that makes them want to attend.

During the shift to adolescence and the transition to secondary school, creating and facilitating an environment that fosters social connection is essential (Daley, 2019), perhaps even more so than the transition to primary school or university.

As young people transition to secondary school, they are seeking new opportunities to be independent and will place less importance on the social connections provided by family, shifting their focus to the new social experiences available within their school. Throughout these transition periods, students will be actively engaging with those outside of their immediate circle, seeking audiences with peers and trusted adults, such as teachers (Allen et al., 2018; Daley, 2019).

Across all levels of the education system, individual schools must be responsible for developing a positive and supportive climate to ensure students have opportunities to connect with their school community. These opportunities need to be designed to create positive associations between the individual relationships they may form with their peers, teachers and support staff, and the environment that brings them all together (Spernes, 2022).

The biggest mistake schools make here is not considering the social experience of their students while designing events and programs to increase a sense of belonging. Social-emotional individuals require an environment that fosters social-emotional fulfilment (Hagenauer et al., 2013). Discounting the importance of friendships and the influence of peers on the overall success of a student in our current education system is placing a ceiling on the level of belonging students can develop.

In schools where students felt that their mental, social and emotional needs were considered, not controlled, and heard by staff in schools, perceptions of belonging, access of school supports and programs, and respect for rules and boundaries increases (Ruiz et al., 2018; Spernes, 2022). In these environments, students not only believe, but see that teachers and administrators care for their wellbeing and their learning equally (Zeinalipour, 2022). They feel like everyone is on the same team and invested in the same goals. Table 3 below highlights ways in which to foster community belonging.

Table 3: Strategies for fostering a sense of belonging

Strategy	Description
Emotional support	Providing emotional support when communicating, especially between trusted adults and young people.
Positive peer culture	Leaders must role model supportive behaviours and align policies and expectations for behaviour and inclusion with teaching social and emotional skills.
Value learning	Create spaces that emphasise the importance and purpose of the material being explored. Share reasonable and appropriate expectations of community members creating learning partnerships.
Be proactive with mental health	Conduct professional development that provides the skills to be preventative and responsive to the mental health and wellbeing needs of the community. Staff should have basic skills to identify problems as they arise and know appropriate referral pathways.
Invite parents in	Parents should have an important role in school communities. Their perceptions of education, and how they value and support the community, will reflect on their children's attitudes and beliefs.

(ADAPTED FROM ALLEN, 2019)

Developing this shared culture of connection in the earliest years of schooling is associated with higher involvement in both class and homework tasks, increased authentic learning and positive social communication and development (Govender et al., 2013). Creating a shared experience shifts ownership and control from the traditional environment of teacher *to* students towards teacher *with* students, a shift that fosters a student's sense of hope and positivity for the future (Zeinalipour, 2022).

Landmark 3: Meaning

"What is the point of learning this? Why are we doing this?"

If you have not heard/overheard this or an equivalent statement from a student, I would start to question your involvement in education. I have had parents lead with a similar statement in a parent-teacher conference, and it has certainly been expressed in frustration in the staffroom. I would guess this line of thinking is pretty synonymous with education in general. The funny thing is the question is valid.

Landmark 3 on the connection journey is meaning, and with good reason. Firstly, it is used interchangeably with purpose, and purpose in our current education system itself is misused and misunderstood. Both meaning and purpose are falsely aligned with future careers, scores, ranks and, ultimately, options that reduce the individual to a cog in the machine (Damon & Malin, 2020).

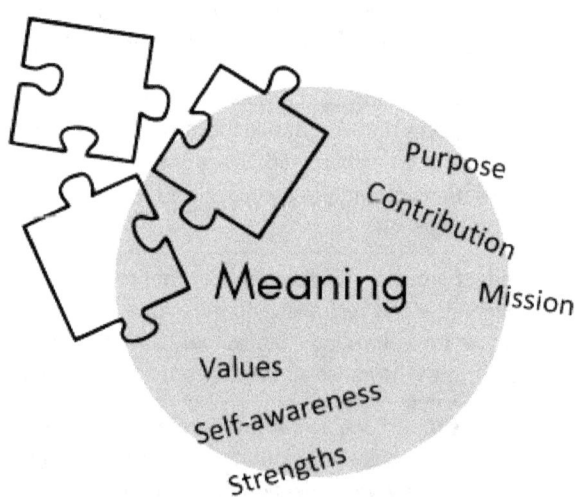

In primary schools, meaning and purpose are used to evaluate secondary schools based on extracurricular programs or average student scores. In secondary schools, they are used to scare students into action, to reinforce the teaching of tired curriculum and to sell programs to incoming students.

What do you want to be when you grow up? is a question designed to inspire children to be curious and imaginative. This, however, is not meaning, yet it is how we treat meaning in our schools. We need to shift our thinking from questioning *what* do you want to be, to *who* do you want to be. Meaning in education needs to be less about the future and more about the here and now. Deep and meaningful connection with others allows us to truly know ourselves.

Schools must shift to developing a focus on assisting young people to know themselves outside of the measurable qualities a degree or a career may require. Educators are spending more and more time building relationships and attempting to learn about their students and, as discussed in Landmark 1: relationships, this holds immense value at the beginning of the connection journey.

The question is this, however, do we, in education, push the students to get to know who they are, what drives them and what they value beyond what feeds the prescribed curriculum or to a depth beyond the superficial? Do we genuinely collect this information for the student to utilise personally or is its primary value in narrowing course selection and pathways options?

Students certainly need to feel as though they have a teacher that knows them and understands their needs (Allen et al., 2018), but not at the cost of knowing this for themselves.

We 'handhold' a lot in education these days, and societal pressures are increasing this phenomenon. A student cannot come to terms with their own meaning without an understanding of who they are and what they are capable of (Rui & Liu, 2023).

> When it comes to creating meaning through learning, we need to *guide more and tell less*.
>
> This means providing:
> - More opportunities for choice, voice and agency;
> - Curriculum that reflects knowledge and skills that are made useful now, rather than in the future; and
> - A shift towards assessment that inspires growth in individuals rather than compliance in cohorts.

When schools do not prioritise connection to the self early, all students are at a greater risk of poor decision-making and increased risk-taking in the future, driven by feelings of social isolation and of hopelessness (Biag, 2016; Peng et al., 2023).

This is a direct disconnect from meaning and provides enormous challenges for schools, especially when a lack of meaning becomes a survival skill.

Feelings of hopelessness can quickly become a learned series of behaviours, initiating the flight, fight, freeze response designed to assist the young person to survive in an environment that may be perceived as unimportant, threatening or not safe (Morton, 2022).

This is, unfortunately, not an uncommon perspective when questioning students on their experiences at school. A young person's meaning within a classroom should not simply be reduced to *survive to the bell*. When it comes to educating a young person, schools are in a pivotal position and are incredibly influential in building not only critical and creative thinking, as well as literacy and numeracy skills, but self-sufficiency, empathetic competence and interpersonal relatedness to those around them (Carney et al., 2017). In Table 4 below you will find some simple strategies for developing community meaning.

Table 4: Strategies for creating a sense of meaning

Strategy	Description
Internal motivation over external achievement	Students should not only learn to complete assessments, but instead discover what they love to do and what the world needs.
Foster collaboration	By working in teams, all community members can develop shared skills and mindsets that are essential to equating actions with a meaningful life.
Coach and mentor	All adults in a school community should be seen as coaches and mentors who share their passions and purposes, and assist others to find theirs.
Connect with the world	Take the class out of the classroom and into the world. Connect with local community environments and connect these real-life experiences to the learning in the curriculum.
Learn from failure	Focusing on grades and performance rankings discourages risk-taking. Create opportunities for celebration of failure as a tool for building perseverance.
Start with why	Working from a values-aligned, purposeful place, hard work does not seem so hard, increasing engagement and enjoyment from the process.

(ADAPTED FROM COOK-DEEGAN, 2016)

Our approach to developing a sense of meaning must be expanded to emphasise and create opportunities for the development of the intrapersonal understanding required for young people to know *who* they are, not just *what* they could be.

The influence of mental, social and emotional development

When a young person is guided on the connection journey, and their experiences at home, school and within the community are relatively consistent, significant protective factors increase naturally (Whitehead et al., 2023). These include, but are not limited to, an increase in a young person's ability to form and maintain respectful relationships, develop high self-esteem and create opportunities for purposeful contributions to their community (Carney et al., 2017; Carney et al., 2020; Lansford et al., 2016).

These young people are much more likely to be considered developmentally healthy, having experienced growth in social competencies such as collaboration and conflict resolution. These contribute then, to increased protection from harms associated with alcohol, drugs, pregnancy and violence (Whitehead et al., 2023). It should not be a surprise that developmentally healthy individuals also perform better at school, both in academic outcomes and in personal development (Lansford et al., 2016).

This, unfortunately, is only applicable to a small percentage of the students who attend schools today. The past few years have certainly seen several challenges that have directly impacted young people (see Figure 4 below), but the percentage of students with challenges in, or a lack of consistency between, home, school and the wider community is large and growing (Jones et al., 2022; Singh et al., 2020).

Figure 4: Psychological distress among 18- to 24-year-olds, by sex, 2007–08 to 2017–18

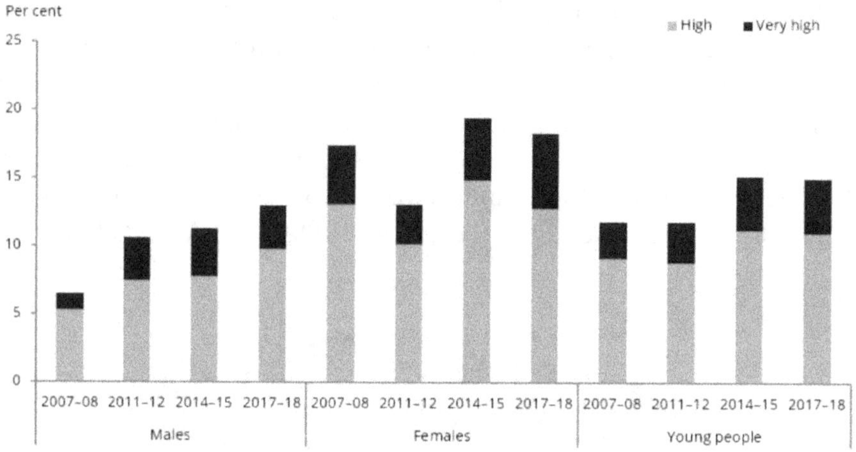

(AUSTRALIAN INSTITUTE OF HEALTH AND WELFARE (AIHW), 2021)

This places the school environment as not only essential in developing skills and knowledge, but also in providing the foundations of connection that may be missing in the other three environments (Whitehead et al., 2023). This is especially true when the schoolyard is both psychologically and physically the safest environment a young person experiences during a standard weekday.

The connection journey has both the ability to impact and be impacted by mental, social and emotional development throughout the time a young person is at school and beyond. Each individual relationship gained or lost will impact the level of belonging created and the space required to identify and work towards meaning.

While the connection journey itself consists of three Landmarks, how the journey looks, feels and is experienced in reality will be dependent on the mental, social and emotional developments that characterise that individual's experience of the lifespan between infancy and early adulthood (Crouch et al., 2019; Goddard, 2021). In a school-aged person, this could mean several quick progressions, quicker regressions, high peaks and low troughs.

A lack of attention to the mental, social and emotional needs of a student will limit their ability to develop a meaningful toolbox of connection strategies. Too much focus may reduce the opportunities for collaboration and the development of support networks among students (Goddard, 2021).

Mental, social and emotional development is a significant determinant impacting the entire connection journey and the sustainability of any success along it. To provide just the right amount of support based on the individual's needs, is to provide the tools and the resources to empower that young person on that day, week or month. If their development is constantly changing, so must our focus on building mental, social and emotional resilience.

Care for a young person at the moment it is needed will change the way in which relationships are formed and the strength of any sense of belonging. But it may be due to time-sensitive factors out of any school staff member's control and, as such, the best course is to adjust intensity but maintain consistent momentum.

In supporting a student to stay within their resilience zone on the connection journey, teachers can create the environment required to turn around a student's day and have significant impact on their connection to the world. Benard and Slade (2009) state "turnaround teachers model and create the nurturing and empowering climates that in turn engage young people's innate resilience" (p.2). In these school environments, students are given the chance to experience connection, increasing the chance of positive developmental outcomes in the future.

Taking the journey

Crawl. Walk. Run.

As a father, I have the incredible privilege of watching my child achieve the developmental milestones of infancy and become more and more aware of the world around them. The sequence in which each skill or increase in cognitive ability directly leads to and builds on the next, is one of the true rewards of parenthood, in my opinion.

Crawl, walk, run is not only a reflection of some very excellent dad memories, but also a mantra for following and taking the connection journey. While a child will progress and learn in sequence, generally following step to step, adults consistently look for shortcuts and easy outs.

I have purposefully called the components of the connection journey *Landmarks* and avoided calling them *stops* for a very distinct reason: you cannot stop at one Landmark or another and successfully maintain sustainable connection. Your progress will be reduced overall, and your initial gains will quickly wither and fade.

> To stop on the connection journey would be to accept that school connectedness is *not a priority*.

To genuinely engage in and follow the connection journey requires constant movement. This is to ensure you keep up with the enormous changes that will occur over time within your community, whether that be people, place or priorities. You need to consistently step out the journey, keeping forward momentum as much as possible and only stop briefly to analyse where you are, what you did to get there and where you would like to go next.

Notice here, that I didn't mention *where you have been*. This is intentional. The world is constantly changing and, depending on your perspective, contemporary schools move either too fast or too slow, but never in sync with the pace of the world.

Because of this discrepancy, the education system spends far too much time worrying about where we used to be and not on where we are, what brought us here and the distance to our next desired state (Bosevska & Kriewaldt, 2020). We need to shift away from constantly looking to the past or too far into the future while embarking on the connection journey. You do not create history by solely looking into the past or having your thoughts firmly focused on the future. You do it by pushing forward with courage in the moment.

Many schools are fantastic at addressing relationships, incredible at establishing curricular and extracurricular activities that foster community and curriculum that inspires meaning, but they treat these in isolation. As the research suggests, connection is not one component, but rather a combination of many, a system of experiences that aligns with actions, values, beliefs and words (Evankovich, 2022). A journey that strikes at the very core of our being.

> The journey involves the optimal development of social, emotional and mental health and wellbeing through:
> 1. The building of strong individual *relationships* and safe, shared social experiences;
> 2. The development of a sense of *belonging*, both self and with others; and
> 3. The identification and understanding of individual and shared *meaning*.

I would wager, many of these components have had some kind of attempt aimed at addressing them in the hope of creating change in your context. Perhaps these efforts have had some or little success in the past. The reason the success was likely limited is bound to the reinforcement of the idea that these components can be treated or managed individual of each other, often by different leaders, with different portfolios or different areas of responsibility.

This individually focused model operates on the assumption that forming strong relationships automatically indicates connection to belonging and meaning (often used interchangeably), which will result in the ideal environment for personal development. In this model, peer-to-peer social experience is not of concern to the whole school and falls under the responsibility of the individual, often labelled a distraction rather than a key component driving positive outcomes.

If you need evidence of this, consider how many conversations you have overheard or participated in, in which friends and friendship groups have been labelled as a core concern rather than a positive contributor to the classroom.

This model places relationships as the sole key to connection and it is a fallacy. One that has led to us drifting from creating meaningful change. If we are to drag ourselves out of the hole we have fallen into, a space where limited research is guiding our efforts to form connection, the journey needs to be carefully mapped out.

The basics of the journey to sustainable connection follow an order in which individual relationships with parents, teachers and students break down the barriers to the wider social experience of learning, working and joining a school community. Once individuals become aligned with groups, the barriers preventing belonging are removed, creating the ideal environment to start thinking on meaning, desire and autonomy.

Connection is fundamentally linked to the school experience because the end point of each is the development of the whole person, complete across the dimensions of mental, social and emotional development. While you can come close by creating your own journey, the research is clear: there is no cheat sheet or shortcut.

There are amazing teachers and education support staff out there who can create incredible relationships with students, parents and their peers. In many cases, they give students a reason to work hard, to commit to conquering challenge and to attending in the first place. These relationships are incredible, but they are not enough.

They are a small part of the connection journey, the first part, and rather than looking at the whole journey, we have been focused on this section almost exclusively. Connection is much more than having a relationship. Connection endures.

Once you have a foundation of relationships, and everyone has some kind of social support, you can then start to build belonging. Once everyone feels like they are part of the whole, they won't worry about the big-picture things and can be free to think about who they are and what their meaning is. Knowing that you are part of a community is empowering and allows you to see its value and alignment with your meaning, leading to stronger and more significant connection.

The connection journey is not a straight line, and approaching each Landmark multiple times is not a measure of failure or regression, but determination and progression. As the school community shifts and grows, so must the road that the connection journey follows. It is not an A to B, but a consistent pattern of creating relationships, to foster belonging, to develop meaning before returning to strengthen relationships again.

When you attempt to circumvent the connection journey, you will inevitably find yourself stuck at building relationships and robbing yourself and others of the chance to create connection that lasts. Relationships are essential, but they are only the beginning of the journey, not the end. If you are finishing at the start, is it any wonder why we are so lost when it comes to connection?

To design a model of the connection journey that was singular and cyclical would not represent the complexity of connecting with other human beings. Each journey will look a little different and be characterised by individual triumphs and tribulations. You cannot skip from Landmark 1 to 3, but you could go from 1 to 2 and back to 1, then 2 to get to 3, such as below:

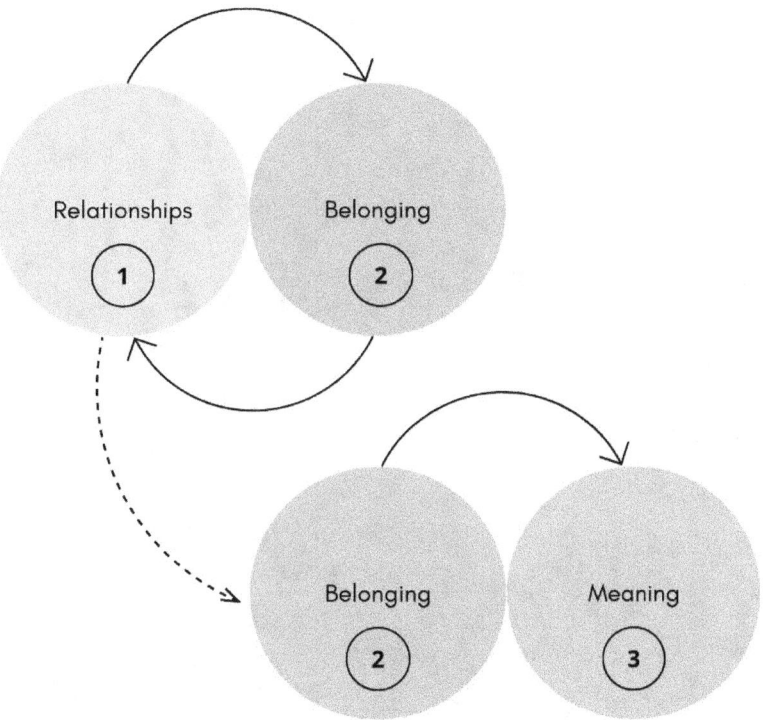

The speed at which you attempt the connection journey is not nearly as important as following the Landmarks and building a sustainable foundation. It may take time, more than you expected, but the journey and the rewards are certainly worth it.

Crawl. Walk. Run.

CHAPTER 2
Non-negotiables

Change is an interesting beast to tame. Often, we feel it is thrust upon us, rather than something we have engaged with, and it is regularly entangled in a wide range of emotional and historical baggage. In this way, it becomes a bit like a tug of war in which things are lost to make way for things to be gained. Being upfront with these challenges is one of many strategies designed to avoid a state in which a community feels the benefits do not outweigh the risks.

This chapter introduces the non-negotiables, a collection of common and frequent factors that may appear as barriers to change ahead of The Connection Curriculum framework. These four factors are not new or revelatory, however, their ability to significantly impact both the change efforts themselves, and the level to which your community engages with the change, is necessary discussion. Next, the need for a new perspective and approach to managing these factors is examined, along with some key questions required to begin the connection journey with your community in earnest.

Cards on the table

I was having a conversation recently and somebody stated, "we are looking down the barrel of some real potential issues with connection in our schools". The statement almost had me fall off my chair.

This was a prominent educational thought leader, somebody I look to for leadership guidance and have the upmost respect for, but they had it so wrong. I should have not been so surprised, it is a statement that is indicative of the education system today. We are typically reactive rather than proactive.

Perhaps few would admit it in public, but it is true. We wait to collect data before we try to positively influence any situation. There are politics involved, of course, but pre-emptive intervention with active monitoring of data would do a world of good for school communities.

We are not looking down the barrel. The metaphorical gun fired a long time ago and we are perpetually chasing the bullets. Perhaps a stronger, more politically correct metaphor is we are chasing our tail, going in circles finding ourselves dizzy and wondering why and where we started. In any case, we are constantly reacting to change because we are constantly behind the eight ball and falling further each year.

Just a year or so ago, we almost looked like we were getting ahead. Imagine, locking schools down and we did a better job of reaching out to each other. Bizarre! Now we are flailing because we cannot accept change in the moment we need it the most. We cannot wait to see what the continued impact of disconnection may bring, to act only then to address a worsened situation.

If we were looking at a potential problem, perhaps this book would not be necessary, or the message would be slightly different. Unfortunately, we are living in it right now and the disconnect is very real. Ignoring the core of the problem with a lack of sustainable action is making it worse.

To embark on the connection journey, we need to reconcile with the fact that it will be difficult and, therefore, requiring a huge collaborative commitment from absolutely everyone in your community, students, parents and staff. If even one of these stakeholder groups does not believe in the need for, the work behind or the benefits of building true connection, the journey will falter.

To embark on the connection journey in earnest with your school community, I (and you) need to first be very clear on some non-negotiable commitments. These are essential components of any successful change implementation and are not unique to The Connection Curriculum framework discussed in the next chapter, but if left unconsidered, these factors pose a very relevant and very real threat to any attempt to create sustainable connection.

Creating the foundation for connection to flourish requires environmental change. Environmental change requires population level change. Population level change requires guidance and some strict commitments to keep the flock from drifting.

> To create the environment required for *sustainable, whole-school connection* to have the greatest chance at success, a school must commit to:
>
> 1. *Constant reflection;*
> 2. *Being realistic;*
> 3. *Embracing the risks;* and
> 4. *Managing effective use of time.*

Addressing these will strengthen any movement towards building and maintaining connection in your context. Honesty, transparency and trust are essential to any community-based change (Winton et al., 2022), and the four non-negotiables should help the train to stay on the tracks through shared accountability.

Clarity and acceptance of these four non-negotiables will ensure a solid foundation for supportive and productive work on the connection journey, reducing some of the common barriers to widespread change, especially a lack of shared norms (Kotter et al., 2021). To ensure that the nature of each is clear, I will expand on the non-negotiables in the following sections.

Reflection = Perfection

Reflection is one of the most essential practices in education. You cannot enact change without it (Kotter et al., 2021). It is one of the non-negotiables, because without a commitment to reflection, you will never build sustainable connection and you will never progress meaningfully as an organisation in this space.

Reflection is how we have managed to get to where we are as a species. Experience, reflect, learn, adapt is literally the process of evolution that has brought us to the point where I can write this book on a device that magically brings our alphabet to life.

One of my favourite authors, Michael Bungay Stanier (2020), in his book *The Advice Trap: Be Humble, Stay Curious & Change the Way You Lead Forever*, details the story of Tenzing Norgay and Sir Edmund Hillary as they summited Mount Everest. To reach the summit requires a huge time commitment and methodical, reflective processes. Two steps forward, one step back. Sometimes one step forward and two steps back. In other words, the process requires acclimatisation (Bungay Stanier, 2020).

Steady progress, patience and teamwork are the name of the game here. You go too quickly, and you risk complete failure. You go too slow, and you run out of resources before you reach your end goal. Like the mountain, connection requires methodical, careful planning and a commitment to reflection and modification, all of which lead to increased chances of success (Bungay Stanier, 2020).

While the process of creating whole-school connection is not as physically or mentally taxing as summiting the tallest mountain in the world, the contributors to success are mirrored in both processes. On the mountain, you may make it all the way to Camp 4, one day away from the summit and need to re-evaluate and return the next season to have the best chance of summiting and returning home alive (Bungay Stanier, 2020). While not life-threatening, I am certain you can think of school initiatives that have pushed for the summit despite obvious signs that the weather was closing in and the results would be forced or, ultimately, detrimental.

While writing *The Connection Curriculum*, I was stuck for a period on how and where reflection belonged. Constant reflection has found itself as part of the overarching non-negotiables rather than a Focus Area, because I do not consider it part of one single action when considering any kind of change facilitation. Rather, reflection is a key component in *how* a framework, initiative or program comes to life (Cameron & Green, 2019).

It is essential that efforts to build connection are accompanied by a commitment to finding the time to reflect often (Cameron & Green, 2019; Flak, 2019). It is not uncommon, despite the knowledge that reflection is incredibly beneficial, for consistent and frequent time to reflect to be missing during the implementation of change initiatives (Burns, 2019; Flak, 2019).

In schools, we often preach to students about the importance of revision and building on success via formative feedback, but lack the self-awareness to create space to reflect on whole-school change ourselves (Burns, 2019).

Reflection at the end of the road is beneficial, however, reflecting throughout the journey is priceless, and ensures that positive heading is maintained and that corrective actions can be made when necessary. Providing this as the only time to collect data towards goals and evaluate initiatives is poor, yet common practice (Kotter et al., 2021).

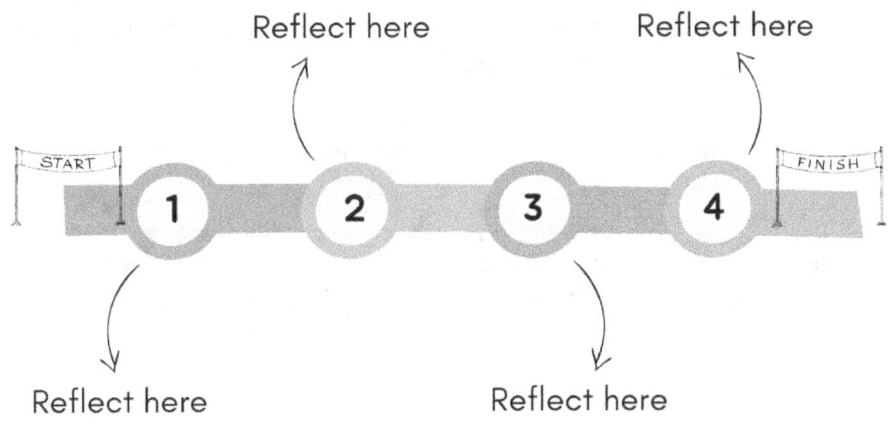

(Reflect at every opportunity throughout your change process)

Frequent reflection is required to avoid knee-jerk actions and to provide the time to ensure all stakeholders and determinants are considered and accounted for (Cameron & Green, 2019). Reflection can be challenging. It requires a level of vulnerability, both of individuals and of communities. Reflection is personal, but if only ever completed individually, we are avoiding the anxiety and accountability that comes with working as a successful team (Wagner et al., 2012). As Cameron and Green (2019) state, "it is only when we are with other people we respect and trust that we really begin to consider other options and look difficulties in the eye" (p.352).

Reflection can stop your organisation from going too hard, too soft, too quickly, too slowly and bringing the whole process to a halt as a result (Burns, 2019). Reflection is what helps your school figure out what is just right for you, and how best to get there with the resources available. There may be quite a lot of work in between this, signs of visible success and what works in your context. Like Goldilocks, trial, error, reflection and persistence will lead to what is *just right* in the end.

The trouble with connection is that any short-term progress may only be *just right* for *right now*. Therefore, we need to constantly be implementing the ideas and strategies suggested in The Connection Curriculum with a whole heap of feedback, reflection and reinvention, and this needs to be more frequently planned for (Burns, 2019; Cameron & Green, 2019).

I finally decided on where reflection fit within the content of this book when I realised that if your school is not ready to shift to consistent, honest and sometimes impromptu assessment of how things are going right now and how that aligns to your goals, you are probably not ready for The Connection Curriculum.

Reflection is non-negotiable, come on back when you agree.

> Simplicity is key when initiating large-scale change. While there are many models to guide reflection, I find that asking the three questions posed by Rolfe et al. (2001): What? So what? Now what? to be more than sufficient in generating meaningful questions, discussion and clarity.

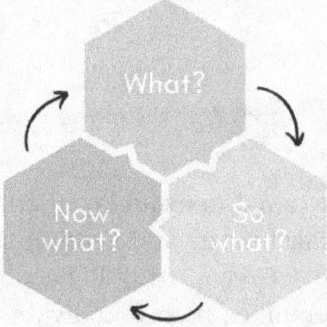

The key is to ensure responses are **detailed** and **descriptive**. We are after deep and clear reflection, not that of a muddy puddle.

Use the following prompts and example questions as a guide:

1. *What?* – Describe the experience in detail
   - What did you observe?
   - What issue is being addressed or population is being served?
   - What did you learn from the experience?
   - What part of your experience was most challenging?

2. *So what?* – Describe why this experience was significant
   - What critical questions does this information cause you to ask?
   - What broader issues arise from the situation at hand?
   - What conclusions can you draw from the experience?
   - How has your understanding of the project/topic/people/community changed because of your participation in this project?
3. *Now what?* – Describe the next steps and how you will approach them
   - How will you apply what you learned from your experience?
   - What would you like to learn more about, related to this project or issue?
   - What follow-up is needed to address any challenges or difficulties?
   - What information can you share with your peers or the community?

Realistic > Idealistic

Schools are full of high ideals. Statements like "catering to the whole child" or "100 per cent inclusive" are littered throughout school policies, websites and marketing materials. High ideals certainly have their place; I would not want to work in a school that was not striving to be inclusive or child centred. But we must be more realistic about how we approach these high ideals in practice and be wary when we are using them to enact movement or motivate action on the connection journey.

Realism and, in particular, realistic goal setting is the second non-negotiable because lofty goals, accompanied by banner-worthy jargon, and wonky implementation plans are too commonplace in education (Carton & Lucas, 2018).

I am not fully committing or admitting to being realistically aligned all the time. We need idealism to be able to dream big and imagine the possibilities within any given situation. Realism relies on idealism to set goals to aim towards and idealism requires realism to get there (Lane, 2017).

Schools, and more widely education systems, need to desperately shift their focus towards a realistic approach to leading, consisting of plans involving short-term goals and long-term goals to meet these high ideals (Kotter et al., 2021).

Simon Sinek (2019) discusses goal setting in relation to the concept of a "Just Cause" – a Just Cause being a specific vision of an ideal future state that equally inspires and motivates action. Sinek's Just Cause is a vision that stands for something, is inclusive, is service-oriented, resilient and idealistic. The Just Cause is anchored in the realistic while aiming for the idealistic. This is not just a lofty goal, that would be too finite (Sinek, 2019). It is a state of infinite adaptation.

When schools operate with their heads in the clouds, setting lofty goals without an understanding of what is happening on the ground, the result is burnout, anxiety and, ultimately, failure (Madigan & Kim, 2021), setting a negative precedent for every single future initiative, program or change process.

We need to shift the lens from the high percentage of idealistic approaches currently the norm in schools and towards a more realistic and, ultimately, context-friendly approach to change leadership. Again, as with reflection (non-negotiable #1), this is not new or startling evidence, it is just missing in action.

Realism as a philosophy of education has existed since Aristotle and Ancient Greece. Through this lens, realists believe that all knowledge is gained through intention and lived experiences. The realism philosophy has endured for centuries because it is the backbone of the way we locate, interpret and analyse information (Erikawati, 2023). It is also one of the key philosophies responsible for the structure of our current school system.

A realist perspective views schools as institutions charged with preparing people with the technical skills and knowledge to be able to contribute to a professional society (Verster et al., 2018). It is structured around curriculum that is "systematic, organised and classified under different subject-matter disciplines such as languages, mathematics, and science" (Tan, 2006, p.24).

Realism has been twisted and misshapen in modern education and now represents measurement, diagnosis, tests and assessments that ultimately value academics, in the most traditional sense, over any form of practical, vocational or experiential learning within a school, and I believe they are wrong in doing so.

Before you comb back through the last few paragraphs to see if you have missed something, I will let you know, you have not. Yes, this non-negotiable is about realistic approaches over idealistic and no, I do not agree with the realism philosophy in the classroom, but I believe that everything works in the right place and realism has a place – just not where it is at the moment.

As discussed in the first non-negotiable, the connection journey requires a methodical approach based on a model of constant reflection. Currently, we build our curriculum around such a model, but do very little to mirror these processes when approaching large-scale change like building sustainable connection.

Whole-school connection is one of those high ideals that is often under-supported by structure and realistic process within schools (Carton & Lucas, 2018). We intend on matching the goal of connection with action, but for the most part they become events, rather than long-term initiatives, and slowly fade into the background, obscured by the shadow of academic achievement and national testing (Allen et al., 2018; Day & Gu, 2013).

In the classroom, a realism philosophy could be controlling and restrictive, however, as a means to structure and control our idealistic goals and initiatives around connection, it may be the key to success. Gone must be the values without action, the mission without progress, and the want to build connection without the sustained, progressive planning to make it a reality.

It is time we flipped the model of schooling making the classroom more idealistic and pragmatic, and the goal-setting processes that support them more realistic. We have the models; we just need to reframe them. There is another book here ready to be written about the failures of the idealistic philosophy of education in today's contemporary landscape, but regarding the connection journey, we need to be much more focused on realism and process, over idealism and vision.

Vision without process is just imagination; we cannot waste more time simply dreaming about connection. It is time to get realistic, it is non-negotiable.

Disable protective mode

Change is difficult and it is our default to avoid it if possible (Suddaby & Foster, 2017). When faced with a challenge, our brain assesses the options, whether we are cognisant of this or not, and makes a series of decisions designed to minimise any harm, as potential or real as it may be (Orridge, 2017). In times of uncertainty, even if we should know we are safe, doubt can creep in and enable our default setting: protective mode.

In protective mode we do everything we can to avoid change from our most comfortable state. We avoid risks, filing through our previous experiences to ensure we participate in activities that have guaranteed results, and we do not engage in anything outside of our normal. It is very much keep-the-wheels-turning-type behaviour.

The third non-negotiable is to disable this instinct; not to turn it off completely, but to reframe our thinking to understand when it is OK to take a risk and when we need to build a little change resilience. Disabling protective mode is essential to the connection journey because we need to fight our instinct to be stopped by the fear of the change necessary to obtain it.

Our brains are designed to create focus among the noise. David DiSalvo (2011) illustrates this tunnel-vision phenomenon by thinking about a picture frame. The frame draws our attention to everything that features within it and obscures everything outside of it. Whenever we look outside of the frame and draw our focus to the details external to our immediate focus, we become stressed, anxious and easily overwhelmed, scrambling to find comfort back within the safety of the frame (DiSalvo, 2011).

If this is sounding at all familiar, then you have clearly been in education long enough to see the rapid rise and eclectic fall of change initiatives in schools. The frame through which we make all decisions in education has become so small and the world outside the frame so great, it has become almost impossible for schools to operate at the pace required to maintain currency in today's world (Wagner et al., 2012).

When it comes to connection, this narrow field of view and shrinking profession-wide comfort zone has led to failed efforts to build positive attitudes surrounding relationships, belonging and meaning. As time goes on, the frame shrinks further and the cognitive biases, or the standards, conventions and characteristics of the decision-maker (DiSalvo, 2011), do so with it.

Failure is the greatest teacher. But it also is the number one contributor to enabling our protective mode and stopping the change necessary in our schools. Connection is not in its own special category here. Numerous initiatives fail, fade or disappear before any action is taken because we consistently fall into the comfort of protective mode, both individually and collectively (Wagner et al., 2012).

Some of this is our natural inclination to make errors when attributing success or failure. When something works, watch the line of people who will happily claim credit for the praise and achievements. When it fails, watch the buck get passed and the blame get shifted to people, luck, resources and the system (You et al., 2021). This inability to share in the value of failure or lack of dedication to pushing through resistance is almost exclusively the fault of our profession falling into the deep pit of self-preservation over acceptance of responsibility, and it is having a huge impact on our ability to build connection at a whole-school level.

Initiatives fail for multiple reasons; sometimes it is due to poor planning, a lack of allocation of resources, difficulties in execution and deficiencies in communication (You et al., 2021). Quite often, it is solely due to people's actions or inactions, fuelled by their perceptions, understandings, concerns and fears, all exacerbated by the need to *protect something*. It could be current workload stress; it could be simply to save face and avoid asking a clarifying question of your leadership. All of it is valid and real and has impact, but it is also limiting, damaging and due to our default to protective mode.

The result of keeping this status quo is, ultimately, a lack of change to the administration of our schools. This resistance to hard change is why forming connection is so difficult now; it is playing against the norm (Bailey, 2014). We have allowed for ecosystems and cliques to form, not genuine connection. Safety in commonality, but that seems very boring to me.

Connection is hard, time-consuming and inherently rife with uncertainty, and we have been trained to avoid these situations, because they might lead to failure, and we might have to admit that it failed one day. In my opinion, this is one of the reasons it is so worthwhile. If connection was easy, it would be automatic. If disabling protective mode was easy, we would embrace resistance and put in the work required for success, every single time.

Time to take risks, disable protective mode and get to work. The changes we make today will form the foundation of the changes we can make tomorrow and, therefore, this is non-negotiable.

> To assist with engaging your community in the change process and starting your connection journey, it is essential that all stages are planned to avoid activating protective mode within the community. John Kotter (2012) created an eight-step model that can guide each stage and keep you and your teams on track.

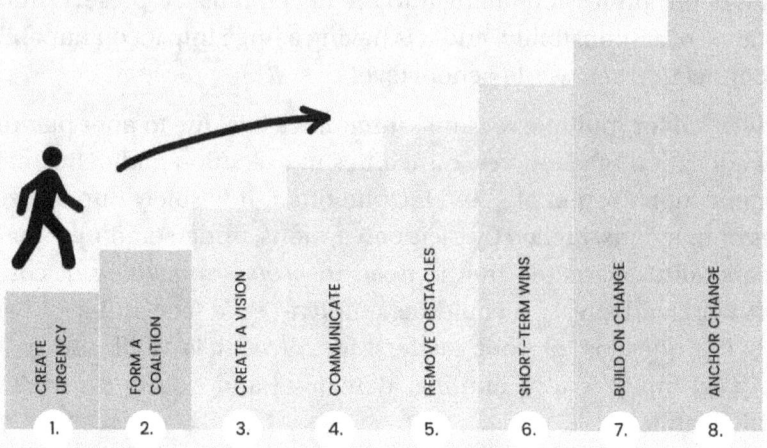

The steps are as follows:

1. *Create a sense of urgency* – Inspire action and build momentum towards connection.
2. *Build a guiding coalition* – Assign a guiding group from people in the community who can work as pillars of change.
3. *Form a strategic vision* – Clarify how this process will differ from initiatives of the past and build buy-in.
4. *Communicate the vision* – Change only occurs when people commit to it! Share the details loudly and proudly.
5. *Enable action by removing obstacles* – Identify and remove the roadblocks to success ASAP.
6. *Generate short-term wins* – Wins must be recognised and celebrated, regularly.
7. *Sustain acceleration and build on change* – Continue to work beyond the first successes and push for more!
8. *Anchor and institute change* – Identify connection between change and success, evaluate and reflect to encourage new behaviours.

Don't talk to me about time

There will never be enough time to complete the numerous tasks required of the modern teacher, administrator or support staff (Stacey et al., 2022). The demands are increasing, too, and this creates a number of barriers to embracing change and building connection; time is just the reigning favourite.

The fact is, though, if you're looking for more time, rather than managing the time you already have, you are responsible for increasing its impact as a barrier and, therefore, making time a limit of progress for yourself. Managing your time effectively is non-negotiable if we are going to genuinely attempt a purposeful connection journey.

Coming to terms with this is difficult – it would be foolish to state otherwise – but it is necessary. Time limitations create artificial boundaries, can limit quality of work, and increase stress and anxiety. None of these are the desired state or result, but they are the reality. Historically, school staff members are often asked to complete more tasks than they have the time allocation to complete (You et al., 2021), and this is not likely going to change in the short term.

You might be thinking, so what can we possibly do?

Well, we need to combat this standard that has been established and fight the instinct to avoid change due to concerns around time allowance (Stacey et al., 2022). Connection is necessary. It is a component of our practice as educators that we have dropped the ball on. Reallocating time will be challenging, but we owe it to the students we teach to make it happen.

While all of this may be starting to sound like an insurmountable hill to climb in your context, the real truth is, this is the perfect opportunity for a boost to whole-school accountability for connection. If you are here and ready to accept that at face value, it is time to jump into the trenches and deal with the real problem behind time as a barrier.

There is, more than likely, a majority in the professional world who respond less than positively to proposals for change, both small- and large-scale (You et al., 2021). When you ask somebody to change, modify or introduce something new to their portfolio or workflow, while expecting a maintenance of results and quality in their existing work, you are fighting an uphill battle (Hay et al., 2021).

We need to focus on prioritising time, scrapping things, leaving things and creating the space for important work to be completed. Once you do this, you can work on setting routines around shared time and working on consistent *use* of time. In her book, *Radical Candor: How to Get What You Want by Saying What You Mean*, Kim Scott (2017) makes a fantastic analogy for changing behaviours and building consistency with of all things dentistry.

Scott (2017) states that we need to stop thinking of change like a root canal and start thinking of it like brushing your teeth. If we do this consistently, every day, making it a part of our lives, then it eventually becomes easy to do and odd if you do not. We need to shift our focus on time lost to building more consistent use of the time we have. The more we focus on doing this, the more it becomes part of our routine and a pattern of behaviour.

Change, connection, managing time... they all don't have to be arduous tasks, especially when we are all working together as a community; in fact, it can be quite manageable (Scott, 2017). We need everyone to be on the same page here, though; everyone needs to understand that if you brush your teeth often, and consistently, you may not need a root canal at all. That sounds non-negotiable to me.

A question of commitment

Movement on the connection journey will require a whole-community approach. Every single person will need to be brought on board in some capacity; you cannot have a whole-school approach if only a small few buy in and participate. To test the commitment of your school or organisation, this chapter introduced the four non-negotiables, a collection of historically preventative concepts that have the power to stop change initiatives in their tracks and that have, effectively, held schools back from creating sustainable progress in a number of spaces, one being connection.

In *The Coaching Habit: Say Less, Ask More & Change the Way You Lead Forever*, Michael Bungay Stanier (2016) highlights seven key questions to help create coaching conversations that foster deep reflection and discussion. I have summarised the core ideas presented by each non-negotiable and, inspired by Stanier's seven questions, created one question per non-negotiable for you and your community to discuss.

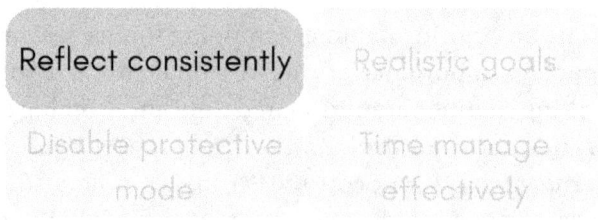

The first non-negotiable is create time to *reflect consistently*.

This is essential to connection as several changes may need to take place in your context to motivate and create movement along the connection journey. While most change initiatives will collect or be influenced by pre- and post-initiative feedback, sustainable change requires a more constant and consistent approach to reflection throughout the journey to account for the dynamic nature of connection and, more importantly, schools. A failure to try, stop, reflect, plan and then continue the connection journey will likely lead to stagnation and very little change from our current levels of disconnection.

Ask your community: *what are the challenges with connection for us?*

The second non-negotiable is to distance ourselves from idealism and focus on *realistic goal-setting* practices.

A vision for whole-school connection is fantastic, but when it comes to action on meeting this vision, schools are often falling short. While idealism has its place, the connection journey requires more tangible and practical efforts to support environmental and structural change. Whole-school connection is a high ideal that needs footholds in reality to be successful. Schools need to plan more effectively for connection and avoid the overuse of educational jargon that plagues and masks poor planning and implementation.

Ask your community: *how will we measure our journey?*

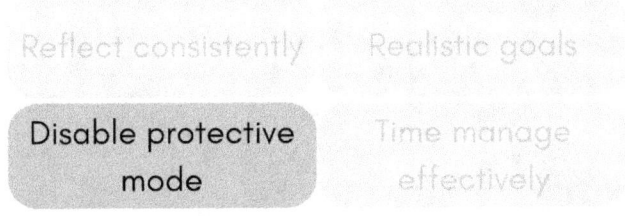

The third non-negotiable is to challenge ourselves and our communities by *disabling protective mode*.

Connection is a hard challenge to tackle; hard change instinctively engages our defences and creates resistance to progress. Schools have slowly adopted a collective protective mode that is stopping progress on the connection journey by maintaining a sense of safety in the status quo. To resist our comfort zone is to engage in the space where ideas are born. Schools need to disable (not remove completely) protective mode and embrace more risk-taking in service of finding something new, different and, hopefully, connecting.

Ask your community: *what are we willing to try?*

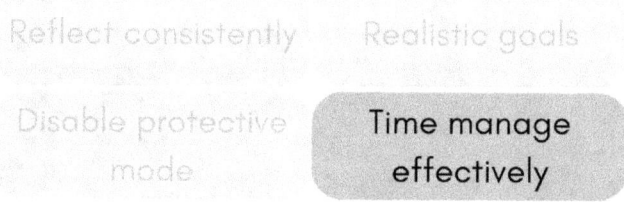

The final non-negotiable is to fight the instinct to use time as a barrier and to *make more effective use of time you have.*

A literal or figurative lack of time can deliver a devastating blow to any initiative in a school, and it is one that has the potential to significantly hamper our efforts to build connection that is sustainable and community wide. Schools must look at the hours, minutes and seconds of the day and align consistent time to developing, implementing, analysing and modifying initiatives designed to create greater levels of genuine connection. Time is a significant challenge, but if we focus on looking at it, rather than looking for it, the size of the challenge becomes much more manageable.

Ask your community: *what do we need to stop doing in order to say yes to connection?*

CHAPTER 3
The Connection Curriculum framework

Educators are a habitual bunch. Although there are exceptions, most schools operate with bell times, rigid timetables and lesson plans, a tribute to the efficiency of traditional schooling. To address the needs of the contemporary school community, a plan of action is necessary. A plan that does not destroy the efficiency in one swift movement, but that methodically and purposefully creates the environment necessary for change and the breathing room required to build momentum towards a school-wide focus on connection.

This chapter begins with a brief discussion of contingencies and their stranglehold on traditional education. These relics of a time past are entrenched in punitive approaches and the reduction of education to a one-way exchange. Next, a discussion of Colonel John Boyd's OODA model unpacks the feedback sequence that supports The Connection Curriculum framework and assists to make informed and contextual decisions. The chapter concludes with an exploration of the framework itself, its three dimensions and six Focus Areas and timely provocations for the journey to come.

A system of contingencies

Contemporary education is built upon a foundation of historical contingencies. *If this* happens, *then this* will likely be the result.

> If you complete this homework task, then you will not receive a detention.
>
> If you study hard, then you will receive a higher grade.
>
> If you receive this score, then you may be offered a university placement.
>
> If you do not meet this requirement, then you may need to repeat.
>
> If you send your child to this school, then they will be successful in this field.
>
> If you complete this training, then you will be a more effective educator.

These contingencies are entirely designed to control and manage, not to inspire or empower. In his book, *Drive: The Surprising Truth About What Motivates Us*, author Daniel H Pink (2011) discusses the nature of *if, then* rewards, and the inherent risk involved in promising to deliver something once something else is completed. These types of exchanges are the backbone of a school's decision-making processes, curriculum design and wellbeing programs, and although they often increase motivation in the short term, their long-term impact often leads to diminishing returns (Pink, 2011).

These types of systems are built on rewarding certain behaviours and punishing others. *If, then* rewards especially are based on soliciting effort, in most cases, against the interests or needs of the individual being asked (Pink, 2011), greatly impacting their intrinsic motivation. As discussed earlier, this focus on what is inside the frame, with its concentration on the finish line and very little in other directions, is limiting the ability of our students, reducing the motivation of our teachers and adding an incredible amount of pressure to school leaders (DiSalvo, 2011).

All of this would be fine if education was a simple exchange between two parties, but it is not a robotic and algorithmic process. True education, also known as learning, requires discovery, empowerment and connection. While there are often pushes for the first two, there is much less targeted focus on the latter.

Contingencies do not foster long-term relationships and, therefore, reduce the connection journey to short-term agreements between people co-existing in the same space by matter of coincidence. Is that a far too harsh analysis of schools? Perhaps, but it is not too far off.

Students attend classes because their timetable, their parents and their teachers tell them to. Teachers take classes because their timetable, their leaders and their pay cheque requires them to. Does this mean that teachers cannot be driven by a passion for their job, or students a love of learning? No. But it stands that the reason people find themselves together and sharing an experience in a school is coincidence.

Not everyone in a school community will be there because they elected to be. Students may attend because they are in the catchment area, their friends are attending or their parents selected the school for them (Abdulkadiroğlu et al., 2020). Similarly, staff may find themselves limited by distance, subjects offered or specific roles. The point here is, we have a system built on contingencies, a community joined by coincidence and a lack of a connective tissue between it all.

Connection is the key, sustainable connection is the goal, and here in this chapter, I introduce to you a framework of three dimensions and six Focus Areas designed to combine both key and goal, while addressing the non-negotiables, and starting your school on a new connection journey.

OODA

There is a growing level of support for a model in education at the moment called OODA (Ryder & Downs, 2022). I think it is brilliant and perfect for my aim of inspiring you to create and maintain sustainable connection. So, I am joining the group as one of those supporters.

OODA, or the OODA loop, created by Colonel John Boyd, a United States fighter pilot and later Pentagon strategist, is a simple feedback model consisting of four stages: observe, orient, decide and act (Donaldson & Harter, 2019; Weger et al., 2023).

Originally designed with the intent of analysing the decision-making process of fighter pilots during combat, OODA is slowly gaining increased popularity in many fields, including education, and not for the comparisons that some may draw between a jet fighter dogfight and a challenging student, despite the memes and GIFs perhaps supporting it.

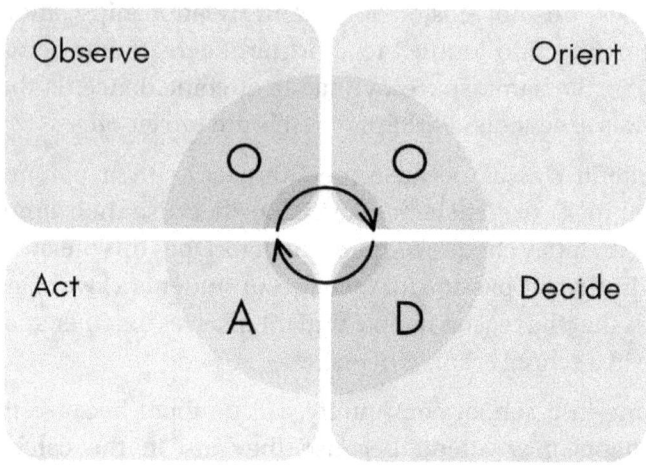

We see a lot of models in education and if you have completed any postgraduate study, then you have most likely seen many more experiential learning examples. When consulting a model, especially through the lens of change leadership, simplicity can be both a burden and a saviour (Weger et al., 2023). On the surface, the OODA loop is simplistic, which could be a red flag, but its value is in its hidden, secret depth, especially within the orientation stage.

If you take the time to unpack OODA, what you will find beyond the four stages is that substantial weight is placed on the orientation stage, to guide and form the perspectives that create our understanding of the environment (observations) and our place within our community (Ryder & Downs, 2022). These perspectives are then fed back into our orientation and help shape our actions, whether that be in battle or in the schoolyard.

Boyd's model has quickly become one of my favourites, and a significant guide to the writing of this book because it is designed around the fact that reality is consistently incomplete. Ryder and Downs (2022) summarise this nicely: "All systems – no matter what form they take – are subject to change, as without change they will soon fall into stagnation and decline. Often, this change can occur in sudden or unexpected ways" (p.6).

I have a huge appreciation for this quote and the message it conveys, because it is so real within an educational context. Far too often, schools will embark on a school-wide effort to create change, with the best of intentions no doubt, but rely on measuring success against a fixed moment in time, rather than understanding the continuous nature of a school's ecosystem.

While OODA is not perfect – and no model will ever be – a continuous feedback loop is the perfect model to align ourselves with in our quest to build and maintain increased levels of connectedness. Success through the OODA loop is not measured by a moment or a milestone, you do not reach the end of the line and celebrate (Donaldson & Harter, 2019). Rather, much like life itself, you must continue to adapt to changes as new information becomes available, then orient, decide and act from that new jumping-off point (Ryder & Downs, 2022).

When embarking on the connection journey, it is essential to consider the four stages of OODA in order to understand the contextual details that create your unique school environment. When we observe, we cannot simply see what is happening on the surface, we must look deeper to view all the angles, the nuances, the stakeholders.

When we orient, we must consider culture, vision, values, previous experiences, new information and the resources we have at our disposal and ones we may need to acquire (Ryder & Downs, 2022). With this information we need to make timely but considered decisions based on the information we have currently and act on this information, while accepting that it will change, and we need to be prepared to constantly change with it, infinitely.

In combat there is an emphasis on speed. Being faster than your opponent is what may prevent you from very significant losses. Following OODA, whether it is combat or classroom, is not about strictly following a set of rules, or flying through to action as quickly as possible (Weger et al., 2023). Speed is important, but the inputs are fluid and as such some loops will be faster than others. The key idea is to complete your observations, orient and make *informed decisions quicker*, supported by the information collated and an understanding of the likely impact it may have on your specific environment (Ryder & Downs, 2022).

Adjust your focus

When it comes to connection, we have been innovating at the margins, focusing on small change rather than those that are more substantial:

- Individual classrooms over whole schools; and
- Relationships as the be all and end all.

We need to adjust our focus and zero in on areas that need, in general, considerably more effort, time and resources than what they have received historically.

At the start of this new connection journey, it is essential you are packed and ready. All four of the non-negotiables have been considered, having guided your inspiration and initial goal setting, and you are ready to start considering the nature of the work your school can – and will need to – do to foster and sustain connection into the future.

It is here that I introduce to you, ahead of a deep dive in Part 2, three dimensions and six Focus Areas that must be addressed as you take the connection journey with your staff, students, parents and local community.

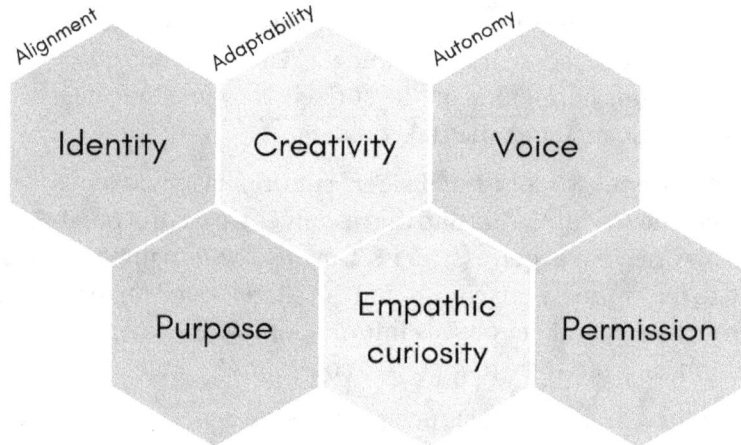

The dimensions and Focus Areas of The Connection Curriculum are the following:

Dimension 1: Alignment.

You can almost certainly create basic connection without considerable effort or planning. This book is not here to discount that fact. Sustainable connection, however, requires a little more effort. Creating the perfect environment for sustainable connection requires a certain level of agreement as to who your organisation is and what their individual and shared purposes are.

To *align* your community will require:

- **Focus Area 1: Identity** (discussed in Chapter 4: Know thyself) in which I question how well your school really knows itself. What do leadership, staff, students and parents say about the school and what is observed? We cannot expect anyone to feel connected if a school community doesn't know *who it is* or is not willing to delve into *who it is not*.

- **Focus Area 2: Purpose** (discussed in Chapter 5: What am I doing?) in which I unpack the application of the final Landmark on the connection journey, meaning. Traditional models of education focus on future application regarding occupation, but is this really allowing students to understand *their meaning*? Without an understanding of their *why*, students can't possibly make deep connections to *what*, *how*, *where* and *when*.

Dimension 2: Adaptability.

Creating any large-scale, organisational-level change requires a community that can identify, meet and work through the challenges that it will encounter on the journey. Sustainable connection requires individuals and groups who can not only problem-solve, but also work with each other to question the status quo and use the answers to create a new beginning.

To encourage *adaptability* will require:

- **Focus Area 3: Creativity** (discussed in Chapter 6: Opportunity creators > Problem-solvers) in which I explore the relationship between connection and instability. Change at scale needs a catalyst. The future needs *disruptors* not *conformists* fixing existing problems, and shared creation is more powerful than shared solution.
- **Focus Area 4: Empathic curiosity** (discussed in Chapter 7: Right in the feels!) in which I highlight that schools, teachers, parents and students need to embrace and create an environment that fosters not just curiosity, but *empathic curiosity*. This creates an environment where people feel safe to discover personal answers to shared questions and welcome everyone else's journey of personal discovery with open arms.

Dimension 3: Autonomy.

Empowerment is essential to the connection journey. Creating a sustainable level of connection that outlives each graduating class or vacating teacher requires connected communities that feel safe to be productive, supported to say their piece and work in true partnership.

Embracing *autonomy*, will require:

- **Focus Area 5: Voice** (discussed in Chapter 8: A seat at the table, not just a sausage in bread) in which I consider the need for initiatives designed to foster connection to be sustainable, distancing themselves from the free dress days and sausage sizzles. Students must also be a

part of school-wide decision-making teams making decisions *with* others rather than having them made *for* them.
- **Focus Area 6: Permission** (discussed in Chapter 9: Houston, we have lift-off!) in which I analyse the subconsciously closed-off nature of schools and the very rare instances in which students, parents or staff have permission to take steps to fully connect and create change in their school. Where is their *autonomy*?

Each of the Focus Areas will be framed through the lens of Boyd's OODA loop, breaking down the research and concepts framing the focus, and the ideas and suggestions designed to motivate your own action in your school. The following subheadings will be consistent throughout these chapters:

- **Tell me!** – introducing the concepts behind the Focus Area;
- **Look for?** – suggestions on what to observe in your context;
- **Which way?** – ideas on how to orient your community;
- **What now?** – keys to framing your decision-making process; and
- **Let's go!** – prompts, questions, future actions to get you moving on the connection journey.

Each Focus Area finishes with the final section titled as above: *Let's go!* This section is designed for you as the individual reading this book. The section is simple and is also not reliant on your role within your school. That means that no matter who you are or what your role is, this is for you. This is how you can have immediate impact despite the readiness of the rest of your community.

It is not a special section for principals, so you cannot excuse yourself as not at that pay grade. It is also not exclusively for the leader or administrator, so you cannot avoid this as the classroom teacher. Whoever you are, if you are reading this book or this section and it inspires you to make change, my hope is that it can help you to make a start and, perhaps, inspire a few others to start coming along with you.

Conscription, not prescription

Before we wrap up and move on to exploring the Focus Areas, I want to conclude this first part of the book with a few reminders and thoughts.

The aim of this book is to empower, not to prescribe.

I want you to join me in a movement of renewed focus on connection, but I can only provide ideas and strategies; the intention is not to tell you step by step how you will build connection, or the choices and decisions that will require. The intention is to encourage you to look at what you have, whether that is knowledge of your people, place and/or process and to empower you with the impetus for change, so you can make choices and decisions that will work for you and for your community.

At its most reduced, this is a book of passionate provocations and a collation of research to support them. When it comes time for you to embark on the connection journey and engage with the six Focus Areas coming up in Part 2, I want you to know that you likely already have the tools. They may be unutilised, old and in poor condition, or even brand new and still in the packaging. You definitely have them, though; I am just encouraging you to use them in a different way, to hopefully build something new with them.

The rest of the book beyond this point is dedicated to breaking down the six Focus Areas requiring your attention if you are committing to change. Like all curriculum outlines, this is a map not a step-by-step guide, and therefore, you should treat it like a map. Not a Google Map with GPS and directions, but one of those old, printed maps; the ones I would produce in Geography classes to a host of groans mixed with astonishment. A map can be inspirational; it should not limit, but unlock all kinds of possibilities.

As we move into Part 2 and the six Focus Areas, I want to be clear about how they are organised. There is no purposeful numbering or organisation of the Focus Areas. Do I believe that these six areas need to be incorporated into your connection efforts? Yes. Do I believe you should attempt them in order? Not necessarily.

But I would encourage you to use the dimensions to help you decide on a starting point. Take a good look around your school and use that information to inform your approach. If one dimension or focus jumps out at you as you read, perhaps this will be the first you look at with your colleagues. If you need to align first, start there. If your school is rigid and inflexible at the best of times, perhaps adaptability or autonomy are the best places to start.

If something is not broken, so to speak – a policy, a program, a structure – do not scrap it entirely, but in the same way, do not accept it as it is now. Strip back to the components that genuinely do work and use them to build something new. You *do not* need to start from zero. Everything up until this point within your school is a part of your connection journey. We do not forget, destroy or demolish. We build and grow.

As you read through Part 2 of this book, look for opportunities to engage students outside their traditional role, look for opportunities to encourage disruption rather than band-aid problem-solving and sticking to the status quo. But always look through your contextual lens:

- Your school;
- Your students;
- Your parents;
- Your staff; and
- Yourself.

We are trying to connect all of them, including you, so they need to be at the centre of it all. No generic recipe is going to work here, unfortunately.

This book is not a turn-by-turn instructional affair. Because, to be quite honest, I don't know what turns you may need to take; what turns you can anticipate; what turns will sneak up out of nowhere. I am confident the six Focus Areas will guide your thinking, planning and implementation. But they are a guide. The journey is all yours.

Take the wheel and start mapping your initial route – not the final one. Not the one that will get you there quickest, that is a cheat. But the first one in potentially many. You cannot finish a race you do not start, so plan and go. See what you find, what it uncovers and what that might tell you about the next leg of the journey. Remember: OODA!

A word of warning, though.

Things may appear closer and bigger than what they seem if you spend too much time looking back. Look back briefly, collect data and turn back towards the now and the immediate future. That is the direction we want to head in, so it is bizarre that schools spend more time looking backwards over forwards and sometimes neither of those directions. You cannot waste time searching for equilibrium because you will never get it.

You will just end up with stagnation and I, personally, have had enough of that for a lifetime.

PART 2
BUILDING CONNECTION

"Invisible threads are the strongest ties"

FRIEDRICH NIETZSCHE

To motivate and create momentum on the connection journey as a community, we must ensure that, like a good hiking trip, we are prepared. **Part 2: Building connection** aims to address the question: *What do I need to develop and maintain sustainable connection?*

Chapters 4 through to 9 detail your packing list for the connection journey through the lens of three dimensions (alignment, adaptability and autonomy) and six Focus Areas (identity, purpose, creativity, empathic curiosity, voice and permission). Each of these chapters will detail the impetus, the theory and provide you with actionable steps towards making your community one that is sustainably connected.

In *Built to Last: Successful Habits of Visionary Companies*, Jim Collins and Jerry Porras (2005) wrote:

> "When in doubt, vary, change, solve the problem, seize the opportunity, experiment, try something new (consistent, of course, with the core ideology)—even if you can't predict precisely how things will turn out. Do something. If one thing fails, try another. Fix. Try. Do. Adjust. Move. Act. No matter what, don't sit still."

Throughout Part 2, with the theory and non-negotiables in mind, this line of thinking guides each of the Focus Areas, which open with a provocation, followed by an exploration via the OODA-style structure, providing the considerations and inspiration to guide your implementation of The Connection Curriculum. Each Focus Area provides your future initiatives the boost they need to create not only strong relationships, but the sense of belonging, and formation of meaning required for true and lasting connectivity.

Alignment

align·ment / əˈlaɪnmənt / *noun*
the state of being **joined with others** in supporting or opposing something.

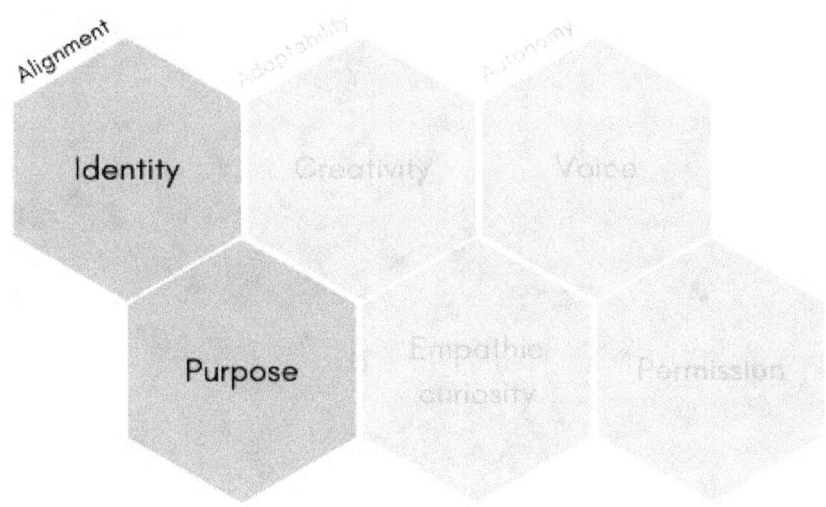

CHAPTER 4
Know thyself
Focus Area 1: Identity

In a connected school it is essential that all members are actively contributing to growth and development, but can only do so with a shared understanding of what they are connected to. The organisational identity of a school is often linked to marketing, and decisions around vision, values and direction are limited to leadership discussion behind closed doors. Opening these doors and creating a shared identity beyond that of academic achievement is crucial to supporting the development of a connected community.

This chapter begins by analysing the typical ways in which identity is experienced, shared and taught in schools today. Concerns with unfocused approaches are explored and a new direction is suggested to bring forth the foundation on which a connected community can be formed. Next, organisational identity is explored through the lens of Haslam et al.'s identity leadership model, coupled with the 5R instructional model to ensure values, goals and direction are in alignment. The chapter concludes with practical suggestions on cultivating whole-community perspectives to develop a shared school identity.

But wait, is there more?

Is your school simply the sum of its parts? While this is usually a positive affirmation, drawing attention to the collaborative strength of a group, with its annual change in student population, is that all a school should aim to be?

Should we limit our schools to simply whoever and whatever, with the foundational identity for the whole organisation changing based on the unique combination of stakeholders for each given year? Or is the strength of a connected community drawn from aligning diverse stakeholders with something they can buy into and share? Turning all your people into members with a shared identity is more likely to bring everyone within it together purposefully.

A shared community identity is just as important as every individual one that connects with it. Schools, curiously, do not often frame discussion around identity with connection in mind. More common is a discussion around image.

How your school is *viewed* is, of course, important data for prospective families, future engagement and for marketing purposes, but it steals the spotlight from vital areas like connectivity.

Image is not identity. Additionally, culture is not identity. Culture is action, it is a visible manifestation of your school's identity and the methods in which you choose to share it. Without an understanding of what you would collectively like your school to be, how can you possibly create a culture to support it?

> **Ask yourself these quick questions:**
> 1. Does your school know what its identity is? How do you know?
> 2. Does the identity differ between current students, staff and families? Does anyone ever ask or challenge it?

Despite what your responses are to the above, whether you had an answer instantly, thought about it for a moment or had no idea how to answer, I invite you to consider this additional question: How can we expect our community to be connected if that same community does not have a shared understanding of who or what it is and, perhaps more importantly, who or what it is not *willing* to be?

Tell me!

There are likely many teachers who are experts at guiding students in developing their personal identities. More commonly, however, students are shepherded into standardised pastoral-type programs that use generalised models of identity strongly tied to academic success (Stahl & McDonald, 2021). Throughout the school years, young people grapple with the changing world around them and how they may fit within it. This development of identity is its own journey, rife with challenges and measured by reflection and experience (Brown & Shay, 2021; Stahl & McDonald, 2021). The worst possible advice a student could receive at this point would be along the lines of *"you are who you are"*.

This is not a positive reflection of identity as a journey and an essential component of connection with the wider world (Stahl & McDonald, 2021). It is incredibly reductive and limits growth and progression to what exists in the here and now. Much like the realities of the connection journey discussed earlier, we must expand our understanding.

'You are who you are' as a statement looks only backwards, limiting your ability to see what is ahead. Who a young person has been should not be a limit to where they could go, what they could become and their identity moving forward (Brown & Shay, 2021).

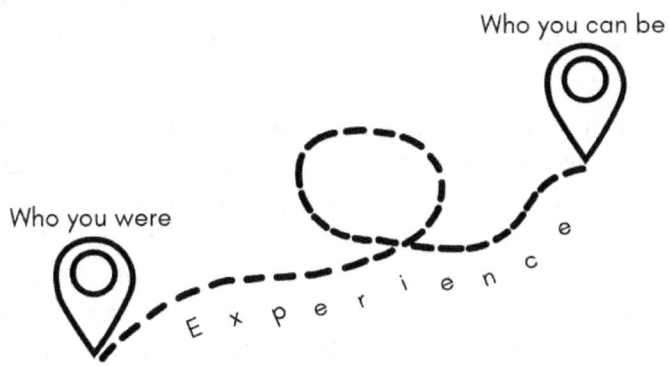

We must understand identity formation cannot be static, it must be understood as dynamic (Fuchsman, 2015). A few pastoral lessons on jobs or pathways are not sufficient work in this space. Identity formation is not a moment in time, but a series of stories being constantly written and collated to form a connected whole (Fuchsman, 2015; Green & Turner, 2017).

Each component is being constantly erased and rewritten based on the shared choices of each member of the community. Identity through this lens is a connective process, rather than an isolated one (Fuchsman, 2015; Brown & Shay, 2021).

A large percentage of young people will develop their identity through experiences in and out of school, through tests of their strengths and reflection on failures (Brown & Shay, 2021; Green & Turner, 2017). This will be automatic. Friends, parents and other family members will all ensure this occurs and shape the directions as it does. Regarding the connection journey, this is only hovering over Landmark 1, the development of relationships.

To create belonging and step towards Landmark 2, it is essential that students, while coming to terms with their own identity, are provided the opportunity to connect to their school community (Green & Turner, 2017). This is because schools are a significant developmental aid when considering a student's personal connection journey, providing their first real-world experiences in diversity, culture, tradition and social development (Allen et al., 2021; Brown & Shay, 2021; Ravasi & Canato, 2013).

The specific combination of these elements within a school community will ultimately determine the features that either broaden or inhibit the breadth of the story that can be written. A focus on developing identity, both individual and shared, forms the foundation for connectivity to a world that is much larger, more complicated and more diverse than they may know (Allen et al., 2021).

With all of this in mind, it is troubling then, to realise that most schools hold the power to creating belonging and, therefore, more sustainable connection, but squander it by neglecting, ignoring or mislabelling their institutional identity (Connolly & Kruse, 2019; Kaptan et al., 2022). Schools need to be more than the broad range of adjectives we can tie to schools defining perceived identity. These are labels for organisation, for ranking and for prospectuses (Connolly & Kruse, 2019; Stone, 2020). Students, teachers and parents may work or send their families to those schools for those reasons, but they are not the antecedents for belonging or connection because they are not something you can necessarily *connect to* (Kaptan et al., 2022).

Like their individual students, a school cannot simply limit itself to *"I am who I am"*, but this does provide a useful first step in understanding institutional identity. If you have a school that markets academic excellence, but data consistently demonstrates otherwise, *know thyself* and be realistic about who you are now and where you would like to be rather than continue to hide behind the jargon, the slogan, the PR (Connolly & Kruse, 2019; Kaptan et al., 2022). It is likely your parents, staff and students already know, so it is time to get real with school identity so that real change can occur, so real connection can occur (Stone, 2020).

Lying to yourself about what your school is at the current moment does not give anyone in your community anything to connect with, or to belong to (Lejeune & Vas, 2014). It will feel disingenuous because it is. Schools need to understand and present their story as a continuous autobiography that provides the history, the present and the desired future honestly (Lejeune & Vas, 2014; Kaptan et al., 2022), no matter how unflattering in stages that might be.

In a school, you want every single person who joins the community to not just read the story, but pick up a pen and add to it. If the story is built on fallacies, you cannot expect connection.

Look for?

1. Heading in the wrong direction!

Schools, particularly those that have been around for a while, more closely reflect the system that governs them, not the context they live and breathe each day (Pitsakis et al, 2012). This is not surprising, as schools are constant offenders when it comes to change, which is often characterised by what is mandated, rather than needed (Beijaard, 2019; Pitsakis et al, 2012).

Contemporary schools, particularly those that chase initiatives and strategies, suffer from a lack of shared identity because their understanding is limited due to the overwhelming number of initiatives being approached at any one time (Beijaard, 2019; Pitsakis et al., 2012). When a school community does not share common identity or direction, despite how incredible an initiative might be, it is very likely to be unsuccessful. When focus is scattered, identity data is shallowly collected and, I should emphasise, not all of this shallow data is actually used, just the *positive* data.

This haphazard focus diminishes a school's ability to address its critical role as a hub of connection and identity formation (Stahl & McDonald, 2021). Identity is not a process that can be solely monitored by numbers and figures, and when it is quantified in this way, the focus is on the result, or an oversimplification of a particular result.

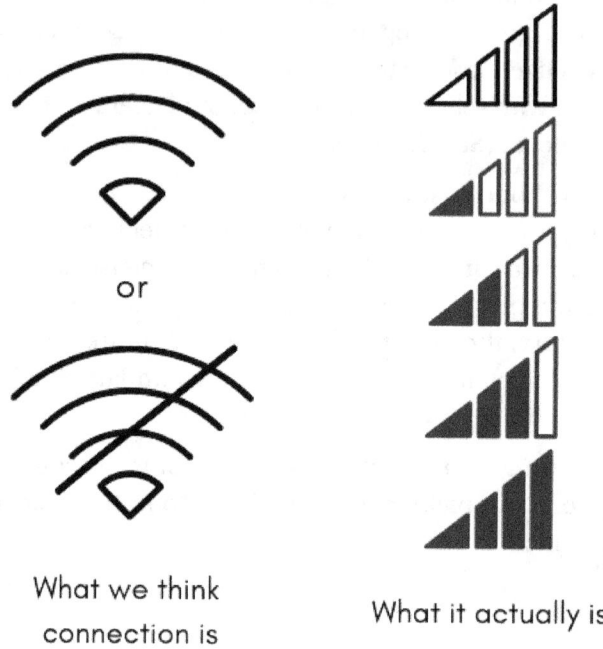

What we think connection is

What it actually is

When we bury identity among a multitude of strategic directions, there is a significant impact on a school community by failing to interrogate and extrapolate the most important data from the individuals themselves, the data that maps the change *you feel across the journey*.

Focus Area 1 wants you to look for opportunities to change your perspective. Stop viewing your community as numbers, percentages and in terms of value add. Find the things that set your school apart from the others down the road and embrace them. Make it meaningful, make it represent currency and make it actionable; otherwise, it is not worth it.

2. Identity linked to achievement.

Too many schools are labelled with or are desperately in search of being a 'high-performing school' (Connolly & Kruse, 2019). A high-performing school is one with great results against significant academic milestones. In Australia this might be National Assessment Plan – Literacy and Numeracy (NAPLAN) or Australian Tertiary Admission Rank (ATAR) scores.

If schools are a significant factor in the formation of identity, and schools continue to model rigidity and a lack of flexibility in the face of new understandings or cultural awakenings, are we really surprised that society also has this difficulty?

The prevailing issue here is that school identity has been limited to achievement, and achievement has been reduced to academic outcomes. If you are an individual who struggles academically (potentially because this has been the focus of your education), are we really expecting you to feel like you have a safe place to belong? If your institutional identity is your shared story, it would be criminal and to the disservice of the whole community to limit this to a median value.

Focus Area 1 wants you to look for the qualities that make your community worth the enrolment other than academic achievement. What can you offer your newest student that brings them closer to understanding the nature of your community and themselves? What can you provide them that will engulf them in the life of the school and bring them closer to establishing the first steps in their shared connection journey?

3. A lack of personality.

It is essential that students, parents and staff not only attend the school, but become a connected member of the community. However, you can only become a member towards something you understand, believe in and, ultimately, can connect to. Herein lies the problem.

Schools are complex environments with many variables and an enormous societal burden to bear (Stahl & McDonald, 2021). This is why control (discussed in many of the Focus Areas of this book) has been the chosen approach to aid with school administration and management.

One of the outcomes of this level and scale of control is uniformity. In a traditional school, uniformity is a benefit – it keeps the pieces in place and the players in check. Uniformity is easy, it's why it has persisted as the model of education across the world (Harber, 2021). It has strength in numbers and easily discounts, reduces or belittles any organisation, collective or institution that tries something different. Think of any school you have ever heard described as 'alternative' and you will understand the bounds of this strict template.

Now, do I believe schools follow the 'factory model' (Darling-Hammond, 2022), turning students into drones and churning out degrees in a consistent and automated fashion? Not quite; it is the right idea, but the wrong focus.

This analogy is perfect for analysing the lack of personality and identity schools have slowly, and perhaps unconsciously, adopted as the scale of education has grown. Students are not drones and staff are not forepersons, but where the factory concept works is in the generic mottos, vision and mission statements that schools produce, reproduce and distribute to the community. These all-purpose lines have constructed an environment that repels the creation of a personalised and shared identity.

Focus Area 1 wants you to look for evidence of cookie-cutter policies, programs, vision, values or otherwise that read well on the page but do not align with your current or desired school identity. Does your school actually value excellence or just results? Does your school value responsibility or do students, staff and parents 'handball' problems until they dissipate or resolve themselves? Either way, redefine, rewrite and realign your mission, vision and values to create the fertile ground required for understanding, belief, belonging and connection to grow.

Which way?

The education system has become the greatest barrier to developing shared identity and sustainable connection. To address this, we need new methods of shared leadership within schools and a new approach to understanding who, what, where and how our community thinks, feels, understands and operates. Haslam et al. (2021a) call this approach the "new psychology of leadership" (p.12), which discards the traditional models in which leaders engage followers through delegation and compliance for those that empower and engage.

This new level of leadership, which is reliant on a foundation of shared social identity, is essential for creating a community of engaged followers and a community that is bound by 'us' and not 'I' or 'them' (Haslam et al., 2021a). The identity leadership model (see Figure 5 opposite) is further enhanced by introducing the 5R instructional model to ensure leadership priorities are aligned with identity priorities (Haslam et al., 2021b). This combination model synchronises identity leadership and engaged followership with the practicalities of the 5R model to create the physical and psychological drive required for shared social identity and sustainable connection (Haslam et al., 2021b).

Figure 5: The identity leadership model combined with the 5R instructional model

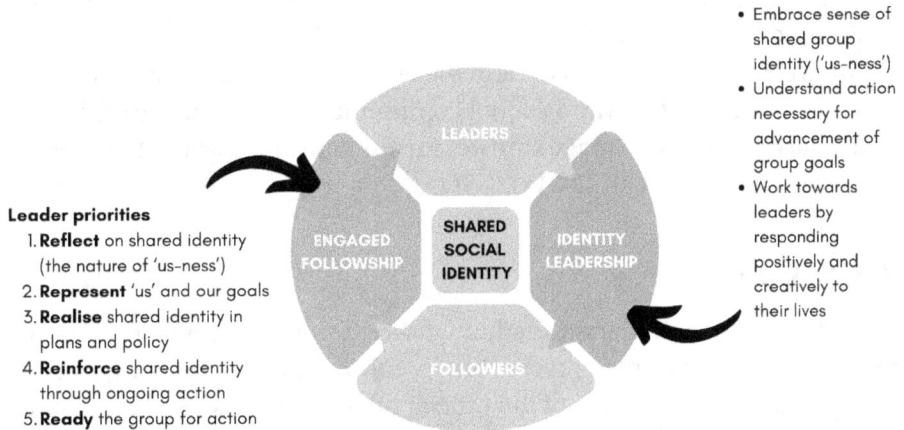

(ADAPTED FROM HASLAM ET AL., 2021B)

The components of the 5R framework are essential when considering this process within a school environment due to the scale of both the organisation itself and the number of potential stakeholders. It is also important to note that while strategic direction and executive decisions may be made by those within formal leadership positions, enacting change towards a shared social identity is a process that does not require formal titles, badges or positions, and all community members should be encouraged to lead and inspire movement towards engaged followership (Haslam, 2021a).

In this environment, community members must be encouraged to become entrepreneurial in their pursuit of connection (Haslam et al., 2017), championing collaboration through:

- *Reflecting* on the current and desired nature of their school identity;
- *Developing* goals, initiatives and strategies that *represent* the 'us-ness' of the school community and the desired future direction;
- *Auditing* and *re-evaluating* school strategic plans, policy and procedure to *realise* the new shared identity and collaborative direction;
- *Reinforcing* shared identity by modelling action, engaging community members and encouraging consultation and dialogue; and
- Swapping leadership for facilitation and creating *readiness* within the community, not only at the beginning of the change process, but throughout, focusing on empowerment, communication and shared understanding (Haslam et al., 2017; Haslam et al., 2021b).

Too often, the decisions made within a school are seemingly against the grain and made in service of interests opposite to those of the greater community (Haslam et al., 2021a). Creating a shared understanding of the goals, rationale and the action required to meet them is essential to creating action within the identity space and the enthusiasm to not only modify and potentially change the way a school community understands itself, but the enthusiasm required to make sure it is meaningful and sustainable (Haslam et al., 2017; Haslam et al., 2021a).

What now?

Fostering a sense of shared identity and realising the challenge set forth in this chapter requires bravery: bravery from leaders, who will need to question the current safety of the official identity of the school, potentially published widely, and known within the community (Nguyen et al., 2022); bravery from students and parents, to speak honestly when questioned, to share opinions freely and become active contributors, a role that may be relatively new to them.

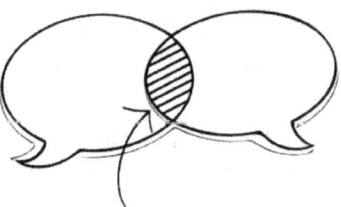

What works for all

To discover the discrepancies that may lead the community in a whole new direction, the community will need to be consulted directly. The town hall model is perfect for this (albeit daunting) for two very explicit reasons:

1. It shows a *dedication* to the cause: this is not an email or a paragraph on the school bulletin about intentions. This is real people coming together to discuss a real community that has a very real impact on its stakeholders. While you can hold these online (the times certainly have changed and safety should be considered paramount), in person will create a greater foundation for future events, of which there will need to be many.
2. It puts everyone in a *vulnerable* position. This may not sound positive, but to openly and honestly share is to be vulnerable. I am certain many

readers will feel the tension in their head and the hair on the back of their neck stand up imagining their community coming together in this forum, but, whether the first, second or third time goes well or not, you cannot assume you know your community and you cannot assume your school represents or caters to that community. You will be miles outside of your comfort zone, but that is vital at this point.

A town hall approach puts people back in the room together and removes the keyboard warriors from play. Should you find your whole identity – print, lived and otherwise – needs a redefine, consult the community on what that may look like. If some of the values are out of date, create new ones that are aligned. If your current identity is right, do not go out of your way to change the framework; change the way you live it. Either way, make it something everyone in your school can connect to, so that they do!

Let's go!

Takeaway #1: Give your community something to connect to.

School communities should share a common identity, something beyond attendance and uniform (Harber, 2021). Every school has an established identity; whether this is positive or lived through experiences at the school is another thing altogether (Brown & Shay, 2021). Adhering to vision and values that have been in place for over a decade is perfectly understandable and acceptable when they align with the current state of the school community. When they do not, they not only contribute to disconnection, but also highlight a lack of contemporary energy and reluctance to change that could be doing the school harm.

Creating discussion around a new identity is a challenge and one that takes considerable time and energy to see through. The benefits, however, could be astronomical to the development of a shared connection journey. While much of this chapter has been an impetus for change, change does not mean a clean slate. Start with what you have if it is going to encourage action in this space. Just remember, when it comes to identity, whether it is based on the current identity you are observing or a completely new one developed through consultation, it must represent your community authentically.

> **Consider the following:**
> Complete an audit of your current school documents (publications, policies, programs and procedures).

- Do these align to shared identity in any shape or form? Is that identity relevant to a 21st-century school, learners or people in general?
  - If so, how can you bring it to life for your community?
  - If not, what can you keep and what can you throw away to make way for new ideas and opportunities?

Look at the current population of your student, parent or staff community.

- What do they need? Why are they here?
- What are the common threads and how can this be funnelled into the development of something that can be shared and celebrated together?

Takeaway #2: Redefine leadership identity.

Schools need a new wave of leaders, both formal and informal; those who have a commitment to learning first and the education system second. Learning is more than books, pens and rows of desks, and leaders within schools are responsible for modelling this to their school community. This new type of leader will pave the way for a new set of priorities, ones that will undoubtedly improve academic achievement, but not ones that make this its sole focus.

These leaders are required because the system will inevitably force the majority back into the safety of the classroom and the uniformity of education at the first speedbump or roadblock (Kaptan et al., 2022). Strong leaders are needed to create the processes (whatever that may be in your context) towards the development of a shared social identity and 'us-ness'. To do this, and to create change towards a more positive, inclusive and collaborative school community, brave individuals and teams must stem the flow of the tide, dig in and push against the resistance (Nguyen et al., 2022).

Consider the following:

Conduct an audit of your most recent strategic plan.

- Does it represent or work to realise shared identity?
- Does it claim to build capacity for connectedness or inclusiveness?
- What could be preventing these from being priorities in your context?

Consider readiness for change in your community.

- What professional or social pressures exist to reduce the impact of any of the 5Rs through leadership practice?
- Is your school helped or harmed by tradition or established practices?

Takeaway #3: Open the doors.

Stop assuming you know your community. Stop making excuses for not getting to know them. Stop giving up on initiatives that involve parents too early, due to poor attendance the first time (a very common occurrence!). Invite your community in, often. Take opinions, thoughts and ideas under genuine consideration and always strive to understand the reasoning behind them.

There is a good chance your community, which may have a love/hate relationship with the organisation, will attend events if it feels a part of the educational process; will contribute to thinktanks and town halls if it believes its opinions are being heard and understood (despite any emotions that may come with them). Staff and students will contribute in much the same way if the doors to offices are truly made to be open, rather than just metaphorically.

Create an environment that has roles for each stakeholder and there will be less confusion, more sharing, more positivity and more growth. A shared community identity will be formed as a result and, if done well, will not require much upkeep to sustain (Stahl & McDonald, 2021). The people will feel connected to it and, therefore, compelled to maintain it.

> **Consider the following:**
> How does your school celebrate/create/sustain shared school identity?
> - Are these events well attended? What is the real purpose behind these events?
> - Are they about community, or are they about something else entirely?
> - Do they contribute to community identity or take from it?
>
> How are students, parents and staff expected to connect with the school?
> - Are any goals linked to identity or community participation working in the opposite direction to these expected roles?
> - Is your school guilty of a convoluted and confusing mission that is impossible to see through to success?
> - How could open-door consultation impact this?

CHAPTER 5

What am I doing?

Focus Area 2: Purpose

We are told from a very early age to start thinking about our place in the world (although not in those exact words) and how we might contribute to the people within it. As a student progresses through our education system, the discussion of purpose shifts from wonder and imagination to career and compensation. The intention of these conversations is to motivate, but this is not the most effective method.

This chapter addresses the mislabelling of purpose within school programs and curriculum, uncoupling the concept from its typical ties to future careers, standardised testing and academic achievement. Secondly, the links between purpose and motivation are explored and a direction suggested utilising Ryan and Deci's theories of Self-Determination and Cognitive Evaluation. The chapter finishes by proposing strategies to take the purpose conversation beyond the four walls of the classroom and into the real world.

Today defines tomorrow

All young people are searching for meaning and to address this, schools dedicate a huge collection of resources designed to focus on future, careers and the discovery of purpose. None of these approaches is inherently wrong, but they are misguided.

Meaning, as discussed earlier, is an essential Landmark on the connection journey, but meaning is also a lifelong pursuit. Young people are less and less concerned with what they *will do* with their life in the future and are more concerned about what they *can do with their lives now*.

Although a very prominent example, Greta Thunberg is a representative of the shifting mindset of young people. There is less focus on 'what they want to be when they grow up' and more focus on 'what the world will *be* when they grow up'. While meaning is an essential component of being connected, for young people, we need to address their sense of purpose and trajectory before we can consider the wider and infinitely more complicated concept of meaning.

Often, these terms are used interchangeably, so I do not blame you if you do not see the difference at this point. Purpose in my mind is fundamentally individual, while meaning is reliant on relationships and a sense of belonging within a community.

At its heart, meaning refers to the overall significance and interpretation that an individual assigns to their life or lived experiences. It is a subjective understanding that gives depth and value to a person's existence. Purpose, on the other hand, is more specific and intentional, providing reasons for one's actions or existence. Purpose is characterised by having clear goals, direction or a sense of mission in life.

To address the needs of young people today, we need to work towards meaning by reinvigorating and revitalising a pursuit of true purpose, focusing less on the future that does not exist and more on developing an understanding of what it means to be the young person they already are, in the world we currently live in. Only from here can we empower young people to start setting lofty goals backed by a strong sense of purpose.

As author and inspirational speaker Simon Sinek would say, we must start with *why*.

Tell me!

What is the purpose of my life?

How can I contribute to the world around me?

When considering purpose in young people, these two questions are the most important to address. They are both simple and dastardly complex at the same time, and infinitely important to both their development and the connection journey (Malin, 2018).

Addressing both questions is essential to defining purpose with any rigor or accuracy, as at its heart, purpose is about a commitment to achievement, both to something that gives meaning to your own life, but also equally contributes to change in others (Araújo et al., 2014; Damon & Malin, 2020; Malin et al., 2019).

Teachers may believe they are equipped to tackle purpose-based education; however, it is not necessarily about your strength as a teacher (Malin et al., 2019). Adults, in a connected community, need more than talent and skill; they first need to be guided by their own sense of purpose. Having a strong sense of your own purpose, and the ambitions and goals it represents, leads to high levels of fulfilment at work, or as a parent and, therefore, a more active role model of having a purposeful life (Malin, 2018).

Purpose is personal and intrinsic in nature, and the way to encourage students to develop and discover their own is not to teach, but to guide (Steger et al., 2021; Stone, 2020). The key is to share your purpose often, frequently exposing young people to the process of setting goals in service of happiness and fulfilment.

From here, ensure that a young person's goals are known and encouraged regularly, despite the nature of the goal itself, with work completed in the classroom always having a component of focus that is beyond the self (Damon & Malin, 2020; Damon et al., 2019; Summers & Falco, 2020; Malin et al., 2019).

Teachers must shift from the driver's seat to the passenger seat when focusing on developing a young person's sense of purpose. Encouragement, feedback and observation are key to highlighting what a student cannot identify in themselves (Damon et al., 2019; Stone, 2020).

This is especially true of any skills, abilities and talents that might build towards purpose and creating meaning, such as self-efficacy, self-esteem, character development and civic engagement (Summers & Falco, 2020). Creating this level of social support is essential for both the individual and their understanding of how far-reaching their actions can be within their community (Damon & Malin, 2020; Malin, 2018; Milner IV, 2014).

The danger in schools currently, is that purpose has become a popular and, therefore, overused term. As a result, its impact is lessened and its definition blurred (Damon et al., 2019; Summers & Falco, 2020; Malin et al., 2019).

Purpose is an educational behemoth when it comes to these 'buzzwords' and is often combined interchangeably with meaning. In this book we build on the foundation of Reker and Wong's theory in which one of the main roles of purpose is as a contributor to meaning and, therefore, it is not the full stop it is often marketed to be (Ratner et al., 2021).

Finding purpose

Separating purpose from meaning allows us to understand what (and how) they each contribute to building sustainable connection. Purpose at its most simplistic is values-based goal setting that creates both the path and the direction for one's trajectory in life, while a sense of meaning is an essential keystone of happiness and thriving (Summers & Falco, 2020; Steger et al., 2021).

Purpose contributes directly to meaning through the process of exploration. The exercise of finding one's purpose requires engagement in a series of intrinsic discoveries around values, morals and interests that then manifest in an understanding of an individual's meaning in life (Malin, 2018; Steger et al., 2021).

Purpose, therefore, is the ultimate intrinsic motivator; the gatekeeper between thoughts and actions. With a strong sense of motivation, guided by a strong sense of purpose, young people can bring their internal desires into the world as tangible actions, leading to an increase in achievement and success (Ratner et al., 2021).

When a student is connected to their purpose, they have a much greater understanding of how they learn best and what they want or need to learn (Ratner et al., 2021). Schools in their current form have stripped students of the ability to learn in a natural and instinctive way, reducing the motive to employability, and securing a particular and specific future (Malin, 2018; Stone, 2020).

To address the pitfalls of this and return a personalised approach to purpose for each learner we engage with, we must focus on the 'why' rather than the 'what'. In doing so we are taking the necessary steps towards creating a deeper understanding of 'how' to get there and 'what' needs to be done to do so (Araújo et al., 2014). Purpose cannot continue to be viewed as something that is an afterschool concern, once the teachers and parents are no longer making all the decisions. Purpose and life do not begin after school ends (Malin, 2018).

When a young person has this arsenal of powerful knowledge in their pocket, they are no longer restricted by the systems built to support their education, and they can truly search for their place within their world and the freedom to have a significant positive impact on it.

Look for?

1. Teaching purpose and avoiding failure.

Those who work in education have some of the most generous souls in the world. As the educational landscape has changed, and the methods in which we live have evolved and developed, the pressure on teachers, support staff and administrators has continued to increase. With increased pressure, especially societal pressure, comes a greater impetus to produce successful outcomes (Milner IV, 2014).

This, although certainly not alone, is one of the reasons for our focus on academic achievement and assessment scores. High scores demonstrate goals, ambition, dedication and purpose. Low scores demonstrate a lack of focus, motivation, drive and, again, purpose. This stigma has been built and ingrained over decades.

The ideal teacher will encourage failure in the classroom, emphasising its value as a learning and reflection tool. However, educators will often hastily teach a student into believing they should focus on a particular study pathway to manufacture purpose, because as adults, not knowing what you want to do is terrifying, especially when a key part of your role is to help a young person make these decisions (Summers & Falco, 2020). This is the key here, though it is not the educator's role to decide on what a young person should, can or will do. It is theirs.

Cape-able of anything

Focus Area 2 wants you to look for learning programs that avoid failure, typeset purpose and designate pathways based on curriculum, electives, extracurricular programs and academic outcomes. The world may be telling schools this is what they should be focused on and how they can best serve their communities, but ultimately, if conformity is not aligned with the school's purpose, then why is it so prominent in the development of the student's?

2. Tunnel vision.

Secondary education, and more specifically the nature of careers education and the methods in which it is marketed, is having a profound impact on the pursuit and understanding of purpose. Pathways planning has become a hot commodity in senior schooling as external organisations, such as universities and specific sectors like healthcare and law, have driven a focus on scores, ranks and minute measures of achievement (Stone, 2020).

This, when coupled with purpose, is incredibly reductive. Purpose is not a job or a career. The firefighter's purpose is not to be the firefighter, it is to help people.

In many schools, the career is sold as the major contributor to purpose (Stone, 2020). This is effective when a student is already driven by a strong sense of career ambition or happens to be receiving assessment outcomes that would open several avenues post schooling.

Where it is predominantly ineffective is for all the other students who may be unsure about the future. Their uncertainty, which should be fostered by enthusiastic guidance from the adults in the room, is met by a distinct measure of concern and sometimes fear. The kind of feelings that make a young person feel they have no drive, no purpose.

This is the opposite environment to what education should be creating. From the moment students enter secondary school, they are expected to exist within the adult confines of the current education system (Malin, 2018), and it is simply not fair.

Focus Area 2 wants you to look for opportunities to break this cycle of career focus = purpose to focus on what the students need to and want to know now, so they can take their own steps towards deciding what they want to do and how they want to get there.

3. Little planting, excessive pruning.

There are many analogies linking the developing brain to cultivating a garden. The reason this type of imagery persists is because it is so valuable as a way of understanding such a complex series of processes.

Young people should spend their days exploring and dreaming – the planting of seeds in the garden. It is essential that many ideas are planted to ensure that the future crop is one that can not only sustain life, but create the fertile ground for further exploration. Because, if childhood and adolescence are the times for planting dreams, adulthood is the time for pruning them (Steger et al., 2021).

While this sounds like a negative, it is an essential part of the process from purpose to meaning. We cannot do it all. Some dreams will need to be pruned and others will need to be watered. The traditional model of schooling is far too excessive with its pruning. Some wild branches should be allowed to stretch and wind. Teachers and parents play a critical role in the premature pruning of dreams and, therefore, the reduction of true purpose (Ratner et al., 2021; Stone, 2020).

As such, Focus Area 2 is asking you to look for this excessive and unnecessary pruning for the sake of a score or a course. While some may see this as essential and inevitable, we must shift towards learning to guide our students more effectively in the discernment of their passions and their aspirations (Steger et al., 2021), to ensure they have the fertile soil to flourish and potentially form their greater sense of meaning.

Which way?

The education system, as it stands today, exists in the belief that if students are taught the knowledge and skills required for specific vocational pathways, young people will develop a sense of purpose and intrinsic drive that will guide them for the entirety of their life (Stone, 2020). This, as outlined previously, is the wrong approach.

Purpose is highly individualised and, as such, it is difficult to quantify within a model. However, when we focus on addressing the environment in which our students learn, we can certainly address their needs and provide them with the guidance required to develop or sustain a strong sense of purpose (Damon & Malin, 2020; Damon et al., 2019; Summers & Falco, 2020; Malin et al., 2019).

Figure 6: Self-Determination Theory

Competence	Autonomy	Relatedness
People need to gain mastery and control of their own lives and their environment.	People need to feel in control of their own life, behaviours and goals.	People need to experience a sense of belonging and connection with other people.
Essential to wellness	This is about choice	Feeling cared for and caring for others

Humans have three basic needs

(ADAPTED FROM RYAN AND DECI, 2022)

Self-Determination Theory (SDT) (see Figure 6 above) is a psychological framework developed by Richard Ryan and Edward Deci (2022) that aims to uncover the origins of motivation and how this may impact on wellbeing, linking closely to the concept of purpose. At its core, SDT identifies three essential psychological needs: competence (feeling capable), autonomy (a sense of control) and relatedness (forming meaningful connections) (Ryan & Deci, 2022). These needs align with the idea that promoting purpose in education involves empowering individuals to take control of their learning journey (autonomy), fostering a sense of capability and achievement (competence) and nurturing collaborative, purpose-driven communities (relatedness) (Wood, 2020).

Within SDT, motivation is categorised along a spectrum from intrinsic (stemming from personal satisfaction) to extrinsic (driven by external rewards or avoidance of punishment) (Ryan & Deci, 2022). In the context of purpose, SDT suggests that individuals are more likely to find a sense of purpose when their motivations align with their intrinsic values and interests. By recognising and supporting these intrinsic motivations, educators can guide students towards discovering their purpose in learning (Malin, 2018).

Cognitive Evaluation Theory (CET) (see Figure 7 below), a component of SDT, further explores how the social and environmental context influences intrinsic motivation. When applied to purpose in education, CET emphasises the importance of creating environments that value individual interests and passions, aligning with the idea that a sense of purpose is often deeply rooted in personal values (Ryan & Deci, 2022).

Figure 7: Cognitive Evaluation Theory

	Non-Self-Determined					Self-Determined
Motivation	A Motivation	Extrinsic Motivation	Extrinsic Motivation	Extrinsic Motivation	Extrinsic Motivation	Intrinsic Motivation
Source of motivation	Impersonal	External	Somewhat external	Somewhat internal	Internal	Internal
Motivation regulation	Not intentional, Non-valuing, Incompetence, Lack of Control	Compliance, Ego Involvement, Internal Rewards & Punishments	Personal Importance, Conscious Valuing	Interest, Enjoyment, Inherent Satisfaction	The team make any final adjustments to the process.	Understand going from people driven to process driven.

(ADAPTED FROM RYAN AND DECI, 2022)

The practical implications of SDT are strongly aligned with the work of schools. Creating an autonomy-supportive environment, where students have agency and control over their learning, contributes to a purposeful educational experience (Wood, 2020). Fostering competence by recognising and celebrating achievements builds confidence and reinforces a sense of purpose. Additionally, nurturing relatedness by cultivating a collaborative and purpose-driven community enhances the overall learning environment (Guay et al., 2021).

SDT not only provides insights into the motivations that drive human behaviour, but also can offer a roadmap (of sorts) for educators to foster purpose in their schools. By aligning with the psychological needs identified in SDT – autonomy, competence and relatedness – educators can create an environment where students are motivated intrinsically, finding purpose in their educational journey through a sense of control, accomplishment and meaningful connections (Guay et al., 2021; Wood, 2020).

When a student has the tools and the support to explore their interests and the freedom to explore these in relation to their values, they are more likely to feel they are acting in line with a strongly defined purpose.

What now?

The one-size-fits-all model of education is outdated and dysfunctional. When considering connection, students need to engage with experiences that shape their understanding of what makes them unique, their strengths, talents, interests and values.

These learnings are essential building blocks towards purpose and, in time, the development of meaning. When this is compounded into curriculum, the opportunities for personalisation of learning are replaced by the 'best practices' that have most recently led to the most desired results. Who is the quantifier of 'best' when it comes to education? Who should have this role?

A school's mission should be to foster a sense of wonder, exploration and an environment that allows a young person to grow based on their passions; an experience that grants autonomy and empowers them to engage in their learning with purpose (Damon & Malin, 2020; Malin et al., 2019). If schools can commit to this change, more individuals within their communities will have a clearer sense of purpose, providing a foundation for understanding why they do what they do, leading to a more profound and fulfilling sense of meaning by offering direction and intentionality to how they do it.

We have the methods and the tools to make this happen in education, but we do not invest the time to developing these avenues to their full potential. It is time to introduce more project-based learning initiatives where students are given autonomy to choose topics aligned with their interests and passions, then change them as the process evolves and develops. This allows students to drive their own learning, fostering an initial sense of purpose as they engage in projects that resonate with their intrinsic motivations. In addition, the collaborative core of these projects develops relatedness, creating opportunities for students to form connections to their community through shared goals and interests.

Schools must increase the scope and scale of how they recognise and celebrate individual achievements. Implementing recognition programs that acknowledge students not only for academic accomplishments but also for their unique contributions, talents and efforts to the wider community, builds a sense of purpose and also increases the growth of connective tissue within the school (Damon & Malin, 2020; Malin, 2018). This approach not only reinforces the importance of competence in the most traditional sense of the term, but also contributes to the formation of a supportive and purpose-driven school community, where each student's distinctive qualities are valued (Milner IV, 2014).

> Sir Ken Robinson and Lou Aronica (2016) summed it up best in their book *Creative Schools: The Grassroots Revolution That's Transforming Education*, stating:
>
> Education should be designed so that students have the opportunity:
>
> *"to understand the world around them and the talents within them so that they can become fulfilled individuals and active, compassionate citizens, able to build lives that have meaning and purpose in an unpredictable future".*
>
> If we are to meet this vision, we cannot keep developing purpose in schools the same way any longer.

Ultimately, teachers who create an environment that respects students' autonomy on their learning journey, contribute to the establishment of meaningful goals, purpose and greater foundation for connections, forming a cohesive and purposeful educational community.

Let's go!

Takeaway #1: Don't lead, guide.

Purpose is part of a greater journey, and we cannot continue to treat it as though it is simply a destination. Young people today require more from the adults in their schools: more opportunities to explore, more opportunities to create the rules around their own learning, and more facilitation and less 'chalk and talk' (Damon & Malin, 2020; Malin et al., 2019; Stone, 2020). Like the greater connection journey, the journey to understanding purpose requires time and support, but it cannot be dictated or replicated across individuals. Less leading students down the path and more guidance from a distance. Learning never happens from the middle of the road; let them drift a little.

> **Consider the following:**
>
> Think of your school community as it is right now.
>
> - How does your school use the term 'purpose'?
> - In what context is it used the most, if at all?
> - Is this useful for the school community or is it tokenistic?
>
> Think of the use of the term 'purpose' by the people in your community.
>
> - How often is purpose discussed outside of academics or careers in your context?
> - Are there particular year levels or periods of the year where purpose is discussed more often? Why and to what end?

Takeaway #2: Purpose is not just about the individual.

We need to embed a greater sense of community within our young people. Purpose is an individualised concept in part, but it should also be more strongly correlated with one's place and contribution to the wider world (Araújo et al., 2014). Students need to develop their intrinsic motivations to create the drive towards their goals, but to recognise their true potential and purpose, we must be creating an environment that assists young people to recognise their place in the world and the impact that position can (and hopefully will) have on everyone around them (Malin et al., 2019).

> **Consider the following:**
>
> Look at your current programs/strategies for the coming semester.
>
> - How do you embed a sense of community purpose in your students?
> - Is there curriculum to support this type of learning?
> - Should there be and in what contexts would this be effective?
>
> Think about the current environment and the people of your community.
>
> - What tools and resources would you need to make a significant change to the way purpose is lived in your community?
> - Do you think it is a priority?
> - Could it be?

Takeaway #3: Change the environment, change the outcome.

School years are formative in relation to purpose. Students figure out what they like and don't like and set themselves on one of the many pathways available to them. Contrary to Malin (2018), schools are trying to accelerate the development and formation of purpose in students much earlier. The feeling is that if students figure out what they want to do earlier, they can set themselves on the 'right' path faster. However, purpose for young people is somewhat dynamic and can change often.

Purpose and the pursuit of purpose is contextual, but we (society) expect them to have it all figured out and this has then crept into school context expectations. We need to change the educational environment to change this outcome. More autonomy, more failure and more relatedness will ultimately lead to a greater sense of purpose and greater levels of connection.

> **Consider the following:**
> Look at the structures and the environment within your school.
> - What three changes could you make to your environment to create increased competence, autonomy and relatedness?
> - How can you make this sustainable and embedded in what you do?
>
> Think about how growth is taught in your school.
> - How often do young people fail in your school?
> - What is the process to support them when they do?
> - If your answer to the first question is on the lower end, what are you protecting them from?
> - What is there to gain from avoidance? What is there that could be lost?

Adaptability

adapt·abil·ity / **ə,dæp.təˈbɪl.ə.ti** / *noun*

an ability or **willingness to change** in order to suit different conditions.

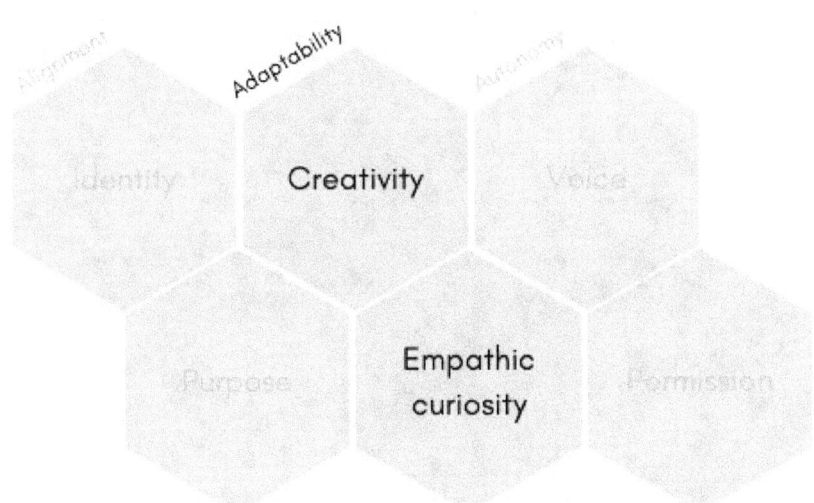

CHAPTER 6
Opportunity creators > Problem-solvers
Focus Area 3: Creativity

Creativity is one of the '21st-century skills' schools across the globe have committed to developing to ensure young people have the capacity to cope with challenges, be adaptative and flexible, and become the solution architects to the problems of the future. The future will need disruptive thinkers to address the growing number of global challenges communities and nations will face, but disruption does not fit nicely within the traditional model of schooling.

This chapter opens with a discussion of disruption as an opportunity rather than something that should be punished or removed. Here it is suggested that students be encouraged to be imaginative and extend beyond the problem-solver to the opportunity creator. Next, creativity at a community level is briefly explored through the Positive Deviance model, in which the traditional hierarchy is challenged to capitalise on the shared creativity of your school. The chapter concludes with a discussion on freeing the classroom of boredom, making learning more applicable to the world, and celebrating disruption.

The imagination thief

Enter 'the problem child'.

[Cue dramatic sting.]

When students are bored, in my experience, they potentially go one of two ways:

1. They quietly *withdraw* from the lesson, retreating to the temptation of a game or video of some description, missing opportunities to explore, learn and *connect* with their peers; or
2. They *disrupt* the tasks being completed. Potentially impacting the lesson, the other students, the support staff, the teacher, they honestly do not discriminate – bless them!

When a student withdraws or disrupts a learning environment, they are automatically labelled a problem. Perhaps not formally or in those words, but they are, because they present a challenge. In a classroom of 27 young people, that challenge can be significant.

Enter 'the disengaged staff member'.

[Cue another dramatic sting.]

When staff – whether they are teachers, support staff, administrators, leaders or otherwise – are bored, they also potentially go one of two ways:

1. They quietly *withdraw*, their boredom failing to fuel their intrinsic motivations and the quality of their practice may decrease. They become disgruntled and frustrated with the profession and some potentially leave; or
2. They *disrupt* to create a change. Fuelled by a need to bring life back into their classroom, they create a burst of motivational effort that can change the way a lesson, staff meeting or student experience looks, feels and *connects*.

When school staff disengage from their work, they become challenging to work with. I have seen incredible teachers and leaders fall victim to disengagement and often when they bring others along with them, it can be highly contagious.

Enter 'the difficult parent'.

[Cue a final dramatic sting.]

When parents are exposed to either or both the previous two characters, it creates concern, frustration and confusion. When a parent experiences this, they additionally can also go one of two ways:

1. They quietly *withdraw*, losing faith in the school and its staff. They may, fuelled by concern and a lack of connection, move their child to another school, or they could become completely disengaged with their child's education altogether; or
2. They *disrupt*, becoming the bane of school staff members' existence. Despite the fact it is likely coming from a place of care for their child, they are labelled difficult and, ultimately, become further *disconnected* from the school community.

It may not resonate with all educators, but when parents react, it is because they care. The way they react is fuelled by how much or, conversely, how little information they have. A connected parent is informed; a disconnected parent is forced to make assumptions.

The design of our current education system encourages stagnation rather than exploration. Questions are asked of these three characters, but often these are intended to have a student return to the work they were bored with, staff to return to the job they are unmotivated to do and parents to blindly support school decisions.

All these situations are opportunities for change and connection, but education has removed our ability to imagine an alternative to the status quo. These situations do not connect people to their work, their peers or their community.

Ed System

Education has become a master thief.

The score: *our imagination.*

Tell me!

When you are able to identify a problem, you are effectively creating a fork in the road of possibilities. There is the first road, one that requires a predetermined solution for passage. The path is light, bright and clear as long as you have a plan, perhaps a modified one from a similar problem solved previously. This path gravitates towards those who like to fix and solve. This is the path of the problem-solver.

The second path is one that requires no plan initially, but does require an openness and flexibility of thought for passage. This is because the path is darker, more mysterious, and the potential problems more clandestine and hidden from view. This is the path of the opportunity creator.

Both the problem-solver and the opportunity creator are incredibly valuable, but only one of them *requires* creativity, while the other simply *encourages* it (Pate et al., 2023). An opportunity creator, also known as a disruptor, sees not only a problem worthy of a solution, but a chance at transforming our understanding of the problem itself (Ramalu et al., 2020). This understanding generates a series of ideas that are intended to not only solve the problem, but eradicate it from existence (Tan, 2023).

Schools are designed to develop students' problem-solving capabilities, but this is completed through the repetitive tasks that lean on standardisation more than they do customisation (Beghetto, 2021; Pate et al., 2023; Tan, 2023). Students are taught to adapt problem-solving experiences from their previous lessons to the new one presented in the latest lesson.

Where this process of learning should be free of guides and constraints, the current restrictive nature of the education system reduces both student and teacher experiences to a series of fetch quests in which all knowledge and skills, including their ability to manage problems, is reduced and limited by a series of interdependencies (Beghetto & Kaufman, 2014; Henriksen et al., 2020; Ramalu et al, 2020; Tan, 2023). Learn A, to learn B, to understand C and D in the later years of schooling.

Connection is investigative, free flowing and supported by our imagination. When we are getting to know someone, we are constantly imagining and forming opinions, thoughts and judgements based on the information we can collect. Schools are reducing the human experience of learning for all involved to a series of numbers and steps, and in doing so, reducing the capacity for true connectivity (Marsh et al., 2021; Mahmoud, 2022).

> When creativity is removed…
>
> *"We fail to spark the delight and magic of learning. We force-feed kids what we ourselves learned, without recognising how different their lives will be. Education persistently focuses on academic knowledge instead of character and skills … and this leaves us in peril."*
>
> Tom Fletcher (2022) in *Ten Survival Skills for a World in Flux: A Practical Guide to the Twenty-First Century*.

When creativity is not a cornerstone of learning, the destination of any school experience is boredom. At its core, creativity has evolved well beyond the individualistic pursuit of the gifted and has evolved into a dynamic and social experience (Mahmoud, 2022). For centuries, the human brain has been developing to enhance our ability to see beyond the world around us, and those who can capitalise, rather than suppress their creativity, are able to create change, not just quick fixes (Marsh et al., 2021).

Edwin Land, a Harvard dropout, developed the instant camera when his three-year-old daughter questioned why she was not able to see the photo he had taken while on a holiday. Polaroid later developed the camera, and the rest is history.

School friends Brian Chesky and Joe Gebbia started a bed and breakfast in their living room with an air mattress, to accommodate visitors who could not find a room in the oversaturated hotel market. Airbnb, Inc. now has over six million listings and owns zero of those properties.

Famously, college dropouts Steve Wozniak and Steve Jobs created Apple Computer in a bedroom at Jobs' family home in the 1970s, changing the personal computing market and pop culture landscape for many decades to come.

The point here is not that a large majority of innovative and game-changing products are developed by people who leave school with great success. These examples represent the value of creativity to our connected world and the need for far more of them in the future (Lassig, 2021; Beghetto & Kaufman, 2014; Remon et al., 2023). Problem-solvers find solutions to an existing problem; opportunity creators find solutions to problems that do not exist yet and push humanity forward (Remon et al., 2023).

Developing an opportunity creator mindset goes hand in hand with creating sustainable connection. The two form an interrelationship in which connected students, staff or parents are more likely to share their ideas, thoughts and opinions passionately and regularly, generating an opportunity for creative thought and discussion (Mahmoud, 2022).

This fuels individual and shared creativity, leading to the development of increasingly progressive ideas aimed at changing the status quo (Remon et al., 2023; Shaheen et al., 2022). When school communities share and collaborate often, it further fuels the connection journey, taking groups from relationships to belonging and potentially meaning, starting the cycle again on a path of exponential growth.

Look for?

1. A reluctance to disrupt.

Change is scary and difficult. If it was not, we would all go and do it, regularly. Most sectors have been through a period of change over the past two decades, some small, some large, some out of necessity, and others to get ahead and stay competitive in a globalised world (Lassig, 2021). Education, unfortunately, is one of a very short list of sectors that has not only, for the most part, avoided large-scale changes, but has actively revolted against them.

Creative endeavours are restricted by an overreliance on summative assessment and ranking, creating a system that does not align with current students and their intrinsic need to play, create and explore (Sahlberg & Doyle, 2019). While the intention may be good, Focus Area 3 is asking you to look for evidence of devaluing creativity by reducing students' and/or teachers' learning to regurgitation in place of creative exploration.

> **A note for leaders:**
>
> Staff either need to be on board or find elsewhere to continue their disruptive and destructive perceptions. Find individuals who stoke this fire and, ultimately, choose your future direction via one of two paths:
>
> - Explain the need for change, use data, use passion, use students and parents. Any who continue to resist, assist these individuals out of the community, creating a greater chance at connection and creativity; or
> - Let them maintain the status quo, one of disconnect, disinterest and disengagement.
>
> It is hard to put out a destructive fire if the fire starters are allowed to *remain and continue lighting*.

2. Structured creativity.

Although educators claim to value creativity, they do not always prioritise it (Henriksen et al., 2020). This could be because creativity becomes difficult through the mountains of regulatory and departmental red tape when it comes to curriculum, or it could be because disruption is not celebrated in a classroom, but often punished. When you consider a disruptive student or colleague, you are most likely thinking of a difficult individual who required significant management, AKA a troublemaker.

As early as our own time as a student, we are shown that it is the teacher's job to control the students and maintain order in the classroom. Unconsciously, this breeds a disconnect between creativity in a controlling, classroom sense and creativity in a wider, more practical, real-world sense. In this environment, teachers can develop an unconscious bias towards creativity based on a fear of disruption to structure (Beghetto, 2021).

A disproportionate focus of recent discourse has been around student management and acceptable classroom behaviours. Not many of these arguments to my knowledge are critical of the structure of a lesson, a unit or of the wider curriculum standards governing the lesson itself. But significant blame has been placed on teachers, parents and the students involved.

This kind of selective vision and a complete unwillingness to admit any kind of fault on the part of system administration is creating schools that believe they are being creative by providing options for submission of a task or freedom of research topic. This kind of work removes any kind of risk-taking and ultimately feigns independence, but plays it far too safe (Henriksen et al., 2020).

Focus Area 3 is asking you to look for evidence of structured creativity, that is, any task, assessment, event or meeting that claims freedom, imagination and creativity, but, ultimately, relies on compliance within an individual's role or workflow. For our parents, students and teachers, outside-of-the-box thinking does not work if you find yourself constantly in an *adjacent box.*

3. Mandated boredom.

This one is easy. Look for bored people.

Teachers are inherently creative people. Yet so many processes in schools create a specific inflexibility that sucks the creativity out of the room (Mahmoud, 2022). These processes are linked to social, emotional, physical and environmental pressures that create a perfect storm of barriers.

These processes are mandating boredom in our schools. They are mandating disconnection in our schools. Are we really sitting and wondering why our communities do not feel a sense of connection to a system that has rarely changed its ways for decades?

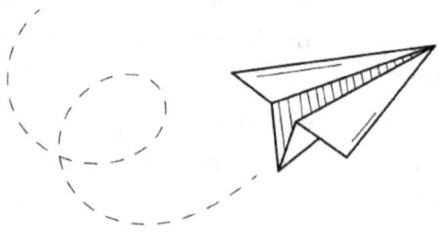

Boredom indicator

Traditional schooling creates bored kids. Quite often discussion drifts towards students being *not the same as they used to be.* This is true. But why should they be? Young people are a product of the world they grow up in. If the world is rapidly changing, why would they not change with it? This is not square peg in a round hole. It is triangle today, hexagon tomorrow. Life is disruptive, surprising and interesting. Young people want to see some of this in their education.

Schools are supposed to be transformative, an institution completely dedicated to the understanding of the world around us and how and where we might fit within it. But schools are not this. You cannot truly connect with a concept by reading it in a textbook or answering an assessment prompt. Contemporary schooling has ripped out application in favour of submission. Students are disconnected from their learning as a result (Remon et al., 2023).

Focus Area 3 wants you to do something I love (sometimes to the awesome combination of eye-rolling and audible groaning): target your bored, disinterested, disengaged students, teachers and parents, and ask them:

1. What about this [topic, task, incident, meeting] is boring? Be specific.
2. What else is boring?
3. What else is boring?
4. Why are these things boring?
5. What would you rather be doing?
6. Why would you rather that? What is its value to you?
7. How can we bring that into this [topic, task, incident, meeting]?

Will this work every time? No, but if you can get through to the final question, the one that asks for the individual to access their creative mind, you could sow the seed for the next interaction, meeting or discussion. Sometimes boredom is exactly what creativity needs; relentless boredom, however, smothers it (Krannich, 2019). Stop treating your bored people like a burden and see them for the fountain of potential creativity they could be.

Which way?

Creativity is controlled in schools because deviance is perceived to be a negative trait in the adult mind. Deviant as a label is often not used positively, but rather to describe something or someone outside of the social norm (Demanet & Van Houtte, 2019). The negative framing is spread socially throughout the world much in the same way we would describe disruption. These two terms do not purely mean disorder or abnormal, and we need to ensure that positive deviance and positive disruption is understood for what it truly is: *opportunity*.

To create change in this space, schools need to address the structure of the traditional decision-making processes that likely govern each move made (Acharya & Taylor, 2012). Adapted from Gilpin-Jackson (2013), Figure 8 below shows a typical decision-making hierarchy commonly found in schools. In this traditional model, decisions are made by school leadership; middle managers implement them; and teachers, students and support staff action them.

A shift towards creativity and connection requires more freedom and empowerment.

Figure 8: Typical vs Positive Deviance hierarchies

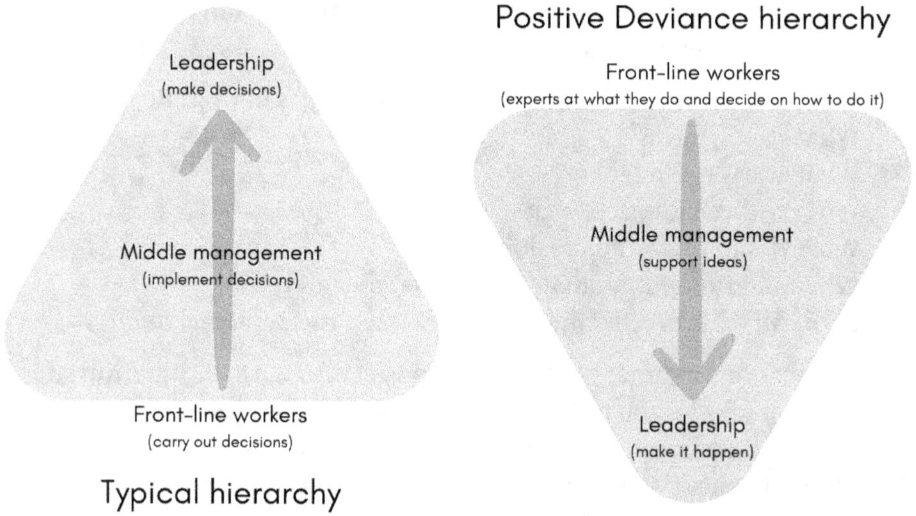

Typical hierarchy
- Leadership (make decisions)
- Middle management (implement decisions)
- Front-line workers (carry out decisions)

Positive Deviance hierarchy
- Front-line workers (experts at what they do and decide on how to do it)
- Middle management (support ideas)
- Leadership (make it happen)

(ADAPTED FROM GILPIN-JACKSON, 2013)

The second hierarchy is based on Positive Deviance, a model that expands on traditional problem-solving, by looking for opportunities to create social change through the wisdom of the change community itself (Singhal & Svenkerud, 2019). In this model, also shown in Figure 8, teachers, students and support staff are treated as experts in their area and are given the space to creatively complete their assigned tasks.

They are free to present ideas and are not simply reduced to drones, mindlessly acting on the decisions of others. Middle managers, rather than implementing decisions from above, now facilitate and support ideas from our contextual experts and feed them to leadership (Singhal & Svenkerud, 2019), who use their position and power to act.

Deviance is typically a failure to obey (Demanet & Van Houtte, 2019). This is all too real in schools. Obey the rules. Obey X because "that is the way things have always been". To create sustainable connection, we must invite unbridled creativity back into our schools and hand the reins over to deviation, to disruption, to imagination.

There are brilliant staff, students and parents in your school community right now deviating from the norm, but because of the structure of education and the way we manage it, this is seen as a negative, or hidden away, shunned as if it is problematic and embarrassing. We see these interactions, initiatives and moments as anomalies because we operate within a traditional hierarchy (Acharya & Taylor, 2012), leading to countless ideas, perspectives and potential initiatives being lost.

It is time to flip the model (literally) and create a community of unrestricted opportunities.

What now?

If your school is claiming innovation or innovative practices, it should be encouraging the abandonment of accepted norms. Decisions should be made using a process like the Positive Deviance model, and hundreds of new ideas should be shared, planned for, implemented and evaluated every school term (Singhal & Svenkerud, 2019).

However, we know this is not true, not yet. Schools need to decide whether they are willing to ditch the innovation label from their marketing or, alternatively, start living up to the claims they are making.

The first step in addressing this discrepancy between words and action is to question: is creativity in your school *mandatory* or *discretionary*? (Acharya & Taylor, 2012). A creative culture is one that inherently shares. Sharing leads to connection.

Establishing creativity, innovation, disruption and deviance as central to the overarching mission of a school is critical to allowing students, teachers, support staff and leaders the space to freely express and showcase their contribution to the community (Remon et al., 2023). Creative endeavours should be celebrated and marked with visual artefacts around the school grounds, and students who question the norm should be celebrated and encouraged to push their questioning further.

Exploratory work should take the place of written standardised assessments, and numbers, ranks and scores should be replaced with play and exploration for primary school students and project-based work for secondary, with detailed feedback and rubrics measuring growth and encouraging goal setting (Johnston et al., 2021; Sahlberg & Doyle, 2019; Pate et al., 2023).

> **Being more creatively minded means asking more questions, essentially:**
> - Curriculum in classrooms should start with questions and time to explore the answers;
> - Parent meetings should start with questions and time to unpack them; and
> - Staff meetings should start with questions and the evidence needed to contextually understand them.

The importance of creativity to a connected community cannot be understated. A culture of creativity is one where outside the box thinking is the default, not the exception.

Let's go!

Takeaway #1: Create and celebrate disruption.

Every improvement we make as a global community is based on addressing a need. The most incredible products and services address needs that do not exist yet. Schools are required to prepare students for a world that does not exist today, and such future citizens will need to deviate and disrupt current processes to survive and thrive (Beghetto & Kaufman, 2014).

If our current efforts to utilise and develop creativity are limited to answering a question, based on a formula, based on a theory, we are having a significant impact on the future – just not one we are intending. Schools should take more time to answer questions, from students, colleagues or parents, with questions, rather than providing answers. Schools should celebrate confusion, failure and deviation from the norm (Remon et al., 2023); the types of environments that foster opportunity creation, not just problem-solving.

> **Consider the following:**
> Think of one common school process designed to manage behaviour, reporting, communication or time.
> - Why does this process exist?
> - How could it be managed differently?
> - What would stop you/someone trying?

Look at the first item on your next meeting agenda, your lead activity for the next class or your go-to starter for a parent.

- Could you change this to be a question?
- Could this add a new dimension to the learning or connection gained from this interaction?

Takeaway #2: Schools need to mirror the world they serve.

The world our students graduate into is one that thrives on creativity, but are our schools fostering true creativity or just grouping visual, physical and design-based skills under a generic umbrella? While there is no doubt these skills are essential to any design or creative process, they are still part of a process (Johnston et al., 2021).

Creativity, curiosity, invention and disruption – none of these when fostered in a genuine and authentic capacity are limited by process. Certainly, they are guided by it, but not restricted by it. Toddlers and pre-school-aged children are at, arguably, one of the most creative and curious stages of the lifespan. They learn to use their imagination to break down walls, rather than put them up (Sahlberg & Doyle, 2019). At some stage during the schooling years, spontaneous creativity makes way for structured creativity and the restrictions of a stagnant curriculum.

Consider the following:

Think about a class you teach.

- What is the most creative endeavour in your classroom?
- What does it involve?
- Do students enjoy engaging with it?

What creative freedoms exist for students, teachers and parents in your context?

- Are they limited? Why?
- Is this based on colloquial evidence or research evidence?
- Are these freedoms in service of assessment or are they in service of learning?

Takeaway #3: Creative schools are connected schools. Connected schools are not boring.

Learning is fun, therefore, education as a framework for engaging young people in the process of learning should also be fun. Education has found itself drift from learning through the engagement of systematic and uninventive methods and a reluctance to let true creativity disrupt the control of the standard operating procedure.

Creativity is stunted because instruction is based on assessment, assessment is based on ranking over growth, and creative endeavours such as hands-on learning programs are half baked and under-resourced (Acharya & Taylor, 2012).

When people are disconnected from their learning, they are disconnected from each other. Education is boring, so school is boring. As a result, students look to create their own fun, their own opportunities. What do we do when they do? We shut it down, restrain their minds and put them back in the confines of the system. We are lobotomising these young people, restricting talented staff and excluding concerned parents.

Not very community-like.

> **Consider the following:**
>
> Think of an experience you have had with one of the three characters from the start of the chapter: 'the problem child', 'the disengaged staff member' or 'the difficult parent'.
>
> - How could you approach this experience differently?
> - Are there traditional structures and processes restricting a more creative approach or resolution?
>
> What is your school's (business's or organisation's) most successful whole-community event?
>
> - Would you describe it as creative or unique?
> - When was the last time it ran differently or introduced a new component? Why?

CHAPTER 7
Right in the feels!
Focus Area 4: Empathic curiosity

Understanding the perspectives and experiences of others must be a priority if connection is to be genuine and sustainable. Current school structures do not encourage enough exploration of human emotion and perspective throughout the schooling years. In a world that is captivated by artificial intelligence and social media, people are the most precious and valuable resource. Connection is how we utilise it for growth and positive community gain.

This chapter starts by highlighting how intrinsically connected empathy and curiosity are and how important it is for schools to focus on developing them in unison. The concept of empathic curiosity is introduced and explored through the PACE model developed by Dr Daniel Hughes, a framework for creating psychologically safe conversations. The chapter concludes with a call to focus on the people within school communities as the most vital learning resource by embracing the most basic of lessons: listen, question, understand, then act, together.

Show your understanding

Curiosity is an essential component of developing the lifelong learner. Young people need their sense of curiosity constantly fuelled to encourage engagement in their learning. For the most part, some may argue that a curious adult is the result of a job well done, but I do not share that belief.

The most curious adults I know found schooling boring, limiting and unimaginative. It was only beyond the school gate that they managed to finally explore the world and home in on whatever and wherever the journey might take them.

Comparatively, empathy is also considered necessary for the development of the lifelong learner. It forms an essential part of most curriculum programs and school missions, yet I would also argue that it is commonly mistaught in many of those school programs. In my experience, sympathy is often more commonly shared through pastoral-type programs under the label of empathy.

This is a problem.

In *Drive: The Surprising Truth About What Motivates Us*, Daniel H Pink (2011) highlights the way we lose curiosity. As infants, we are inherently curious about everything in our world, especially the people around us. Our brain is wired to absorb as much information as possible about those people to feed the incredible growth that is occurring throughout all the body systems, but particularly in our brains.

Babies six months to a year old all revel in this default setting of curiosity. It is only when we reach schooling age, and particularly when standardised assessments and chairs in rows become the norm, that something switches us off our default curiosity-driven mode. Out of default mode, as we age, we draw further and further away from being inherently curious about the people within our world and more focused on our own world happening in front of us.

Is it any wonder then, that schools could be struggling to teach empathy? How can you demonstrate empathy when you are not curious about the people you are interacting with, or with their experiences, their circumstances, their beliefs?

I have overheard it said that young people lack empathy and curiosity; well, I wholeheartedly disagree. If that were the case, to be honest, it is likely because we are teaching them that is the way. The connection journey is built on the foundation of relationships, but within a school these relationships cannot be limited to the small few you are friends, classmates or colleagues with.

Ambitiously, we are aiming to connect the whole community and, as such, we need to aim for more. In this book, when we discuss the need for schools to connect, we are not simply discussing how to find ideas and satiate your own sense of curiosity. We need to be more curious about the people around us and, therefore, a focus on curiosity alone is not sufficient.

Curiosity is valuable to the connection journey, but to connect those people to others, we must link it with an understanding of empathy. It is time to bring them together in the name of connection and shift our focus from isolation to combination, just like the individuals in the communities we are trying to connect.

Tell me!

Empathic curiosity is genuinely and compassionately acting to understand a person's views, beliefs and perspectives to understand their actions, decisions and past experiences (Dahlström et al., 2023; Han et al., 2023; Nadelson et al., 2019; Nazir & Lin, 2023). To demonstrate empathic curiosity, an individual must avoid the temptation of comprehending only the words being spoken, and instead seek to comprehend the feelings and motivations behind the words, promoting the formation of deeper connections (Dahlström et al., 2023; Han et al., 2023).

In schools, where the diversity and size of the community can be incredibly varied, empathic curiosity becomes an essential component in the supportive relationship required between teachers, parents and students (Dahlström et al., 2023; Zurn & Shankar, 2020). Empathic curiosity transcends shallow, surface-level interactions and encourages discovery, learning and an appreciation for the strengths, challenges and aspirations of all in the community (Gorny-Wegrzyn & Perry, 2021; Nadelson et al., 2019). Ultimately, this fuels the journey to sustainable connection through the cultivation of stronger relationships, belonging and inclusivity.

In a way, empathic curiosity becomes the adhesive that binds a community together (Magrì, 2020). While a typical approach to connectivity may involve phone calls, emails and parent-student-teacher conferences, this is often not about exchanging understandings, but communicating data in a unidirectional manner.

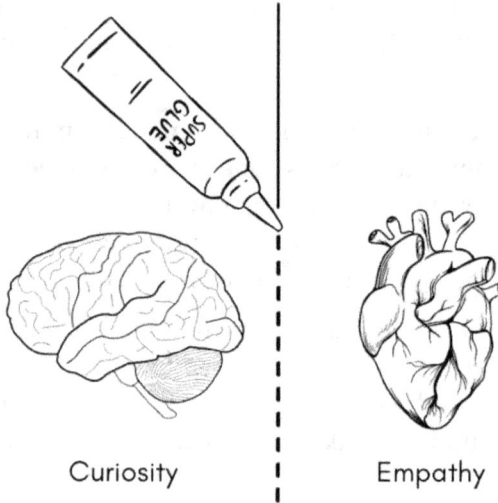

Curiosity | Empathy

The stronger the effort a school makes towards empathic curiosity, the stronger the links between stakeholders, and the stronger the potential for connection (Zurn & Shankar, 2020). Schools are in a prime position, as a community connection point, for introducing an empathically curious approach, in which all community members develop, and are exposed to, varied views, motivations and understandings (Dahlström et al., 2023; Magrì, 2020; Nadelson et al., 2019).

When school leaders and teachers, who are primarily responsible for guidance regarding academics, are provided the space to go beyond their role as curriculum providers, they become mentors and role models of empathy and curiosity (Nadelson et al., 2019). When parents, who in many cases feel isolated from their child's schooling experiences, can actively participate, they gain a greater understanding of teaching and its challenges, opportunities and intricacies (Mayseless & Kizel, 2022).

This curiosity creates a supportive connection between both the school and the home environment, where understanding opens the door for extension of the learning experience to outside of the classroom (Stern, 2018). This realignment of purpose through a sharing of perspective allows for teachers and parents to become partners in the support of the young person (Mayseless & Kizel, 2022; Stern, 2018), strengthening the relationship between home and their school.

This connective tissue is essential, especially for adolescents as they attempt to navigate the social, emotional and intellectual challenges during this stage of the lifespan. Developing supportive relationships and a sense of belonging is essential during this period (Mayseless & Kizel, 2022).

Where teachers can provide an environment in which students' perspectives are acknowledged and valued, education extends beyond the traditional model of schooling, where classrooms become spaces where curiosity is fuelled and a lifelong connection to learning is fostered (Buheji, 2019).

Empathic curiosity addresses the traditional roles of an educational community, roles that while well understood as antiquated, post-COVID-19 have seen a resurgence out of a need to spark stability and control. As a result of this, it is essential that the exceptional teachers seeking connection within their community become the role models for a future of education that nurtures empathic curiosity and deep investment in the humans, not simply their capacity for absorption of prescribed knowledge (Berkovich, 2020; Buheji, 2019; Stern, 2018).

These educators, armed with an innate sense of empathic curiosity, seek to understand the young people in their care, involve the parents for their valuable insight (Golding, 2017) and consult with their colleagues to build a true, sustainably connected community (Berkovich, 2020) – one that effectively blends the cultural, familial and individual perspectives that make it unique, valuable and worth celebrating.

Look for?

1. Parents outside the gate.

Connection with parents is a proven method for improving student outcomes (Mayseless & Kizel, 2022). Schools that manage to work in partnership with their parent body are much more effective in creating a sense of true community.

Parents who feel they are a part of the process are much more aligned with the decision-making approaches, the values and the expectations set by their child's school and, as such, are a resource rather than a burden. While much of the connective tissue between a parent and a school is through their child, limiting all contact to this – at times – potentially unreliable messenger, is troublesome to say the least.

While some parents can be considered 'difficult' to manage for a plethora of reasons, one of the primary antecedents of conflict or poor relationship-building is isolation. Although perhaps a generalisation, as an educator,

I must believe that the majority of parents want to be effective in their role as primary carer for their young people.

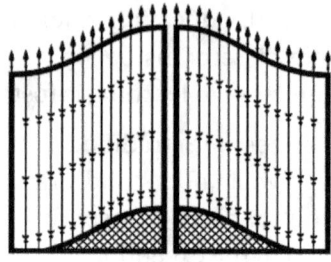

Parent trap

In the earliest days, parents have complete control but as the child begins school, they start to lose this oversight and, if not supported, can feel completely withdrawn from the development of their child (Stern, 2018). Focus Area 4 wants you to look for opportunities to engage with your parent community beyond the contact that typically sounds like:

Your student A, has been involved in X, Y, Z.

Create events for parents to attend beyond those explicitly linked to the actions or performance of their young people, and invest some time, some resources and (my advice) some food towards truly connecting the adults on both sides of the student.

2. A lack of genuine collegiality.

Secondary schools, with their subject-specialist staff – potentially in subject-specific offices – are encouraged to work in silos. In primary schools, particularly large ones, this may also be the case, despite the departmental mandates of collaboration and interdisciplinary focus.

Teachers who build strong relationships in their subject areas create strong curriculum, role model positive interpersonal skills for students, and increase staff satisfaction in the workplace (Buheji, 2019). These silo success stories, however, do very little for whole-school connection.

While the silo may be the best solution for planning and delivering high-quality lessons in a subject area, the strength of the team can become cliquey and isolating for both those in the group and those outside of it. While the common solution is to bring all staff together for professional development or staff briefings, these overly structured occasions create very little space for the genuine sharing of opinions, beliefs and perspectives.

Focus Area 4 is asking you to look for chances to break the structure and provide teachers and school staff more widely the opportunity to celebrate and be together as a larger group. Make it physical (but not exhausting), fun and do it offsite. Break down the barriers by connecting on neutral ground away from the silos and the labs, fields, studios and workshops that inadvertently support them.

3. Screen-to-screen communication.

Digital tools have afforded us an incredible array of resources to communicate widely and instantaneously, but have they connected us truly? Within a school, the digitisation of communication channels in some respects is revolutionary as the potential audience has widened and the amount of content that can be shared has increased dramatically.

In many cases, the electronic newsletter, digital consent form and online booklist has saved a considerable environmental and economic cost, but other methods of communication such as email over phone call and phone call over face-to-face meeting are only serving to separate the human aspects of a school community to create a false feeling of time reclaimed or effort saved.

The most connected communities I have worked in have set boundaries around digital communications. The best example of this, in my opinion, was anything longer than a 10-minute phone conversation should be dealt with face to face. You may read this and cringe or shudder at the time spent for this to occur on both sides of the table, but the reality is, it is extremely difficult to develop empathy digitally when compared to sharing a space in person.

Restricting contact home to phone calls or emails is particularly damaging to forming a sense of community between the support systems inside the gate and outside of it. Focus Area 4 wants you to look for opportunities to modify your policies regarding contact,* both inside and outside of the school. Empathic curiosity needs genuine moments between people to lead to connection (Golding, 2017; Han et al., 2023; Nadelson et al., 2019). While it might be 'costly' to set a meeting initially, the potential for connection in the long term is certainly worth the commitment.

---

* No, I have not completely lost the plot. Do not change every email or phone call to a face-to-face encounter, but try to look for more moments where the positives connection-wise outweigh the costs timewise.

Which way?

To create a sustainably connected school community, we must improve the way we build the foundational relationships necessary for the journey. We can do this important work by redefining the way we communicate and collaborate with all members of our school communities (Golding, 2017).

American psychologist Dr Daniel Hughes created the principles of the PACE model (Playfulness, Acceptance, Curiosity and Empathy) (see Figure 9 below) primarily to promote psychological safe conversations between adults and young people (Golding, 2017; Hughes & Golding, 2012). In developing a framework for schools to create a culture that thrives on the empathically curious connection between parents, students and teachers, the PACE principles can provide a scaffold for reimagining the social contract of the modern school.

Figure 9: PACE model

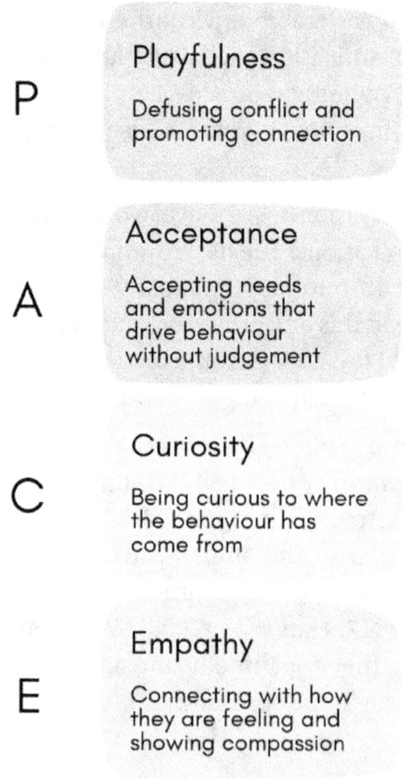

P — **Playfulness**
Defusing conflict and promoting connection

A — **Acceptance**
Accepting needs and emotions that drive behaviour without judgement

C — **Curiosity**
Being curious to where the behaviour has come from

E — **Empathy**
Connecting with how they are feeling and showing compassion

(ADAPTED FROM GOLDING, 2017)

To address *Playfulness*, schools do not need to look to the work of stand-up comedians or teach their lessons exclusively through play (although, why not?). Playfulness through the lens of whole-school connection relates to positivity (Hughes & Golding, 2012). Leaders should look to abandon the typical contact to staff, parents and students that highlights concerns and issues consequences (Golding, 2017).

The negative framing of these interactions does little to highlight the supportive nature of the school, despite the best intentions. While consequences for actions are necessary and behaviour curriculum important, discussions – especially with parents – should not exclusively be through this negative frame (Golding, 2017).

The entire community should embrace a positive, reflective and restorative style to their communications that is constructive, but growth focused (Hughes & Golding, 2012). This encourages open and friendly interactions among parents, students and teachers.

Acceptance in a connected school embraces inclusivity (Hughes & Golding, 2012). This is not just addressed by the teaching and learning programs, although inclusivity in this space is essential, it is about developing a culture that emphasises the fundamental contribution that each student, parent or teacher brings to the school community.

Acceptance ensures that each individual is connected to the whole via an understanding of their unique talents, skills and qualities, and is utilised actively so they can contribute and grow with the young people learning (Golding, 2017). Regular acknowledgement and celebration of the diversity within the school and the surrounds is essential in developing belonging and continuing the connection journey.

Curiosity is the skeleton on which education was born. Students are not the only learners in a school community, however, and it is essential that all members are given the opportunity to grow through the shared connection with the school. Each student, as well as their parents and their teachers, should feel empowered as a member of the school so that everyone is confident to ask questions, share their perspectives and openly communicate about their child's education, its challenges, as well as its successes (Hughes & Golding, 2012).

Providing the chances as well as opportunities to learn through workshops for adults and children alike will advance the school community along the connection journey and develop a culture more reminiscent of continuous and curious learning.

Finally, to demonstrate *Empathy*, schools need to step outside of the standard awards, subject selection and performance nights. Each of these have their place and celebrate essential parts of the community, however, they do not facilitate conversations that uncover experiential understanding.

A school should celebrate its story, both formally and informally, with occasions that highlight the history, the diversity and the personalities that form it. Many schools have extensive alumni networks; these types of supports, with their celebrations and services, must be extended to the whole-school community so that families, staff and students can connect with, and enrich, the living school community prior to milestones such as graduation. The greater the shared understanding, the greater the empathy, the greater the connection (Golding, 2017; Hughes & Golding, 2012).

What now?

In *Dare to Lead: Brave Work. Tough Conversations. Whole Hearts.* Brené Brown (2018) quotes Minouche Shafik, the director of the London School of Economics, regarding the future of employment:

> "In the past, jobs were about muscles, now they're about brains, but in the future they'll be about the heart."

Brown (2018) believes that individuals who are successful in the future will need to work closely with others, to support the human aspects of the new world of work. As artificial intelligence and automation continue to develop and rapidly expand, humans will perform less of the routine work and more of the complex social and emotional work the machines cannot do (as of yet!).

Empathic curiosity is developed with use, it is a learned set of skills and, along with the wider umbrella of emotional intelligence (Dahlström et al., 2023), must be a focus of the education system moving forward in both curriculum and otherwise.

It is the otherwise that will lead to greater levels of connection. Spontaneity should be a part of learning, but it certainly is not a part of education. Tom Fletcher (2022) in his book *Ten Survival Skills for a World in Flux* states:

> "Globally, we seem to be in a period when there is too much certainty and too little curiosity. People are finding themselves drawn further into echo chambers, in which they hear only the views of those with whom they already agree."

Schools have an incredible opportunity to combat these echo chambers by utilising the communities they belong to more effectively. There are very few other periods of time where such a potential collection of people, backgrounds, ages, demographics and experiences could be brought together so efficiently than those within the schooling years (Buheji, 2019).

Even where the mean years of schooling are low, the same opportunity exists, but the timeline is shorter. It makes no difference, because the time for developing the empathic curiosity and emotional intelligence of not only the young people but the adults within your school, is now. Whether you will be connected directly for three years or for 13, there is no time to waste.

The greatest asset to your connection journey is the others around you, and the same can be said of growth. When a school can develop a culture of community-based learning, there are no longer parents, teachers and students. Only learners. Learners with different skill sets, different stories, and different social and emotional value.

Empathic curiosity is the key to unlocking all that potential. Schools, school leaders and teachers must begin to realise that kindness and empathy are not a consolation prize from a good education – they are central to an exceptional education (Fletcher, 2022). Where strategic and annual implementation plans speak of wellbeing, outcomes and community (and I am certain they all do), you must consider empathy and curiosity as the pillars of your approach.

Stop obsessing over data such as results or satisfaction levels, and start focusing on the people providing the data, their stories and their valuable perspectives.

How do we do it? Fletcher makes it simple: "observing, learning, practising and teaching".

The new curriculum is *people*.

Go explore it.

Let's go!

Takeaway #1: Do not only listen with your ears.

True connection is more than words. When you are communicating with others in your community, do not only listen with your ears and the words being spoken, but actively listen with your heart (Brown, 2018; Golding, 2017).

Don't just hear the words. Feel the meaning behind them, and the intention behind the individual sharing them with you. Across all community members, listening with the heart will create environments of greater understanding, will unlock the real, deep and meaningful questions that need to be asked, and will foster greater levels of connection in the process.

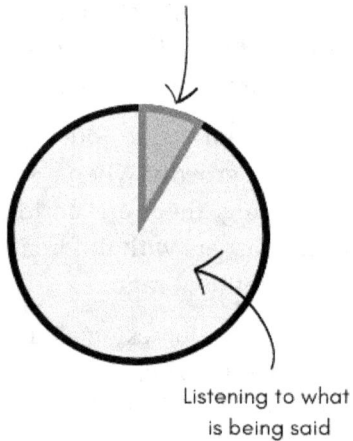

When we (really) listen

Consider the following:
Think about some recent professional conversations you have had.
- Do you often lose track of the conversation because you are thinking of your next addition, retort or opinion?
- Could you learn more about the others in the room by listening and not saying your piece?

How can you help students/parents/colleagues to listen with their heart?
- How might you frame your next conversation with one of these people to ensure you are understanding the feelings behind their words?

Takeaway #2: Be more childlike.

Children ask unlimited questions and infinite follow-up questions to those initial questions. To learn more about the individuals in your community – your students, colleagues and the parents – ask more questions, just like a child would (Zurn & Shankar, 2020). Be more curious about those around you, especially when they are outside of your usual circle. Children do not worry about whether their question is of a particular quality, they just ask (Zurn & Shankar, 2020). There are no stupid questions when the question is genuine, respectful and well-intentioned. Do not spend time worrying about the question. The question is the shovel, the potential answers are the gold.

> **Consider the following:**
> How do you ask for questions in your leadership positions or in parent meetings or in your classroom?
> - Does this method work?
> - Do you role model empathic curiosity?
>
> Think about whole-school/staff gatherings.
> - Have you desperately held on to a question in the hope someone else might ask in your place?
> - What is lost in these situations?
> - What could be gained connection-wise if you asked?

Takeaway #3: Be the mirror and reflect.

Empathic curiosity requires time and active engagement, no matter your age. To ensure you improve your active listening, responding and understanding, you must be reflective in your practice (Stern, 2018). It will be illuminating, it may be shocking, frustrating and definitely awkward at times, but we are all human. No matter what, try and then: reflect, reflect, reflect.

> **Consider the following:**
> Do you set aside time to reflect on difficult conversations?
> - Do you keep notes or ask others for feedback?
> - If not, what potential learning could you be missing?
>
> Think of a time when you have reflected on a conversation that went poorly; one where you learned a potential reason as to why it may have occurred in this way.
> - Could this information have assisted you to engage more empathetically or curiously initially?
> - How can you take this experience and apply it to future conversations?

Autonomy

au·ton·o·my / ɔːˈtɒnəmi / *noun*
the ability to act and make decisions **without being controlled** by anyone else.

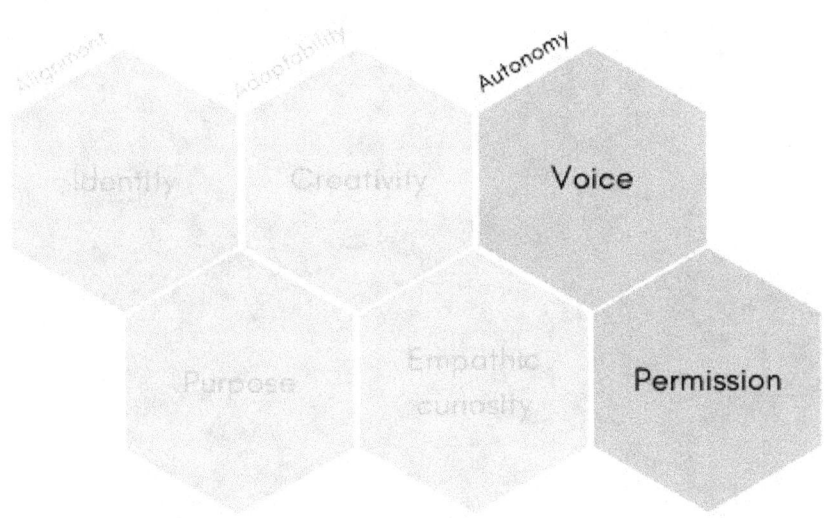

CHAPTER 8
A seat at the table, not just a sausage in bread
Focus Area 5: Voice

School hierarchies are not often designed to allow young people to engage outside of the parameters of the typical student. Schools are run by adults, and this is the reality for several reasons, however, in a connected school, decision-making can be a partnership. Young people are much more capable than they are given credit for and opportunities for them to prove this are essential in a connected school community.

This chapter opens with an analysis of the issues surrounding student voice and a clarification of what it both is and is not. Next, through the models developed by Professor Laura Lundy and Gerison Lansdown, the discussion shifts to creating an environment in which authentic and sustainable practices are introduced to increase the influence of students alongside the adults within the community. Finally, the chapter calls for a shift to the traditional power dynamic that results in tokenistic and disingenuous initiatives that encourage passive rather than active participation.

All sizzle, no substance

Australian schools have a history of some truly awesome barbecues for community events. I distinctly remember as a primary school student lining up for the right of passage that was the standard supermarket sausage, served in a slice of cheap white bread, with tomato sauce poured from a three-litre container. Fantastic.

The sausage sizzle is an Australian staple and a clear favourite for fundraisers, parent evenings and sporting carnivals. A sizzle, and other events like it, certainly bring people in the community together, but it does not keep them connected. A gold coin for a sausage can get the best of us up and through the school gates for an information night, but it is a quick, delicious, fleeting moment and not a long-term solution.

Similarly, staff in schools often have morning teas to celebrate milestones, birthdays and the start/end of terms. These are great and they certainly bring staff together. But how often do they manage to break the cliques and the faculty groups? Staff may be together in the same room for the same purpose briefly (party pies and sausage rolls in my experience), but they do not spend the time connecting as a whole group any more than if morning tea was delivered to separate offices.

This is not the connection you are looking for

Schools often provide the token community events like the sausage sizzle as they believe they are bringing everyone together and strengthening the community. Often, they do bring people together, but not in the meaningful way we want in a connected school. Students especially are offered the token event like the sausage sizzle instead of the opportunity to connect with their school and the empowerment and confidence to influence change in their environment.

Now, don't get me wrong, I am not saying *boycott the sizzle*. They have a delicious place and, for better or worse, are an important part in our education history. However, when a sausage sizzle, a free dress day, a welcome banner or a special edition of the newsletter are in place of efforts that would provide space, audience, voice and influence (Lundy, 2007) to all community members, especially students, they are unfortunately doing very little other than being a delicious disservice.

Tell me!

This section begins with a fact: adults have controlled the education system and students have had very little to do outside of a passive participatory role (Hands, 2014).

The world perceives young people as being characterised by resistance, rebellion and failure to conform to adult-moderated societal norms (Yuen, 2022). Through this lens the scepticism surrounding student voice finds its roots. When these perspectives are presented in the media and mirrored by political leaders and academics, students are labelled as problems needing solutions rather than contributors towards solution (Yuen, 2022).

Connection as a concept is not solely concerned with student voice, however, the distinct lack of genuine student contribution, especially when it comes to change management, is hard to ignore. Community voice is the ultimate goal in a truly connected school, but until we address the exclusion of students from the decisions that shape *their* education, we are not likely to obtain it.

Focus Area 5, therefore, is primarily focused on bringing the young people in to sit with the adults, whether they be administrators, board members, teachers, parents or concerned neighbours (Hands, 2014). They need a seat and an opportunity. Once we can accept our students as more than recipients of education and as contributors to shared learning, we can then move on to parents and the wider community, but we must be methodical.

The critics of student voice typically perceive a dramatic shift in power or, more accurately, a loss of power, rather than a sharing of influence and expansion of learning (Cook-Sather, 2020). This is a critical misunderstanding of the concept according to Cook-Sather (2020), who emphasises student voice "does not aim to replace the presence and power of seasoned practitioners and certified professionals but rather to legitimate alongside those experts the experiences, perspectives, and expertise of students" (p.4). These negative perceptions have historically excluded students, despite their place as essential stakeholders within a school community; after all, what is a school without its students?

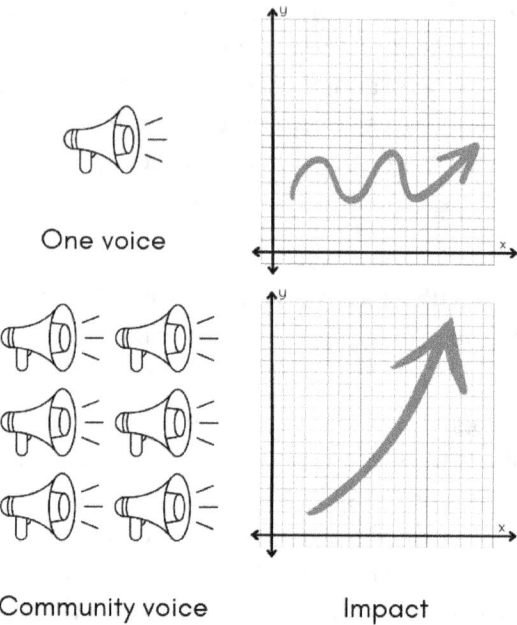

Researchers have determined that students are an abundant source of valuable insight and should not be placed on the fringe of the decision-making process (Lac & Cumings Mansfield, 2018; Weiss, 2018). When this is the shared perspective of school leaders, the school community is impeded from designing and implementing effective change (Weiss, 2018). Such a mindset removes a student's ability to be an active contributor in their learning and exacerbates the regularity at which students describe their educational experience as anonymous and helpless (Yuen, 2022).

This exclusion is essential for understanding the importance of introducing sustainable connection initiatives in schools. Students should have the right to form and share their own views, despite whether that view is correct or praiseworthy (Shier, 2019). Within schools, the curriculum being taught, the teaching quality and policies that support those processes have a significant impact on the young person, however, students are rarely afforded the opportunity to share their views in an official capacity (Shier, 2019).

Schools can be alienating environments for their students (Yuen, 2022), and those high levels of alienation lead to disengagement and the drastic reduction of attendance, self-concept, academic achievement and an increase in school dropouts, fuelled by a narrative of distrust and inequity (Lac & Cumings Mansfield, 2018; Mitra, 2018).

Approaches to student voice address the question "who is setting the agenda, on what terms and in whose interests?" (Shier, 2019, p.2). School leaders, administrators and teachers have a responsibility to listen to those who are impacted by their practices the most (Cook-Sather, 2018).

> Treacy and Leavy (2021) suggest both staff and students require dedicated professional development to ensure that each group can contribute to the change process. While considerable professional development structures already exist in many schools, student voice should become a priority for all stakeholders involved.
>
> If the goal is to encourage staff and students to form a partnership and have significant influence on the schools they belong to, both parties require training and coaching to effectively organise, discuss, plan and action change initiatives.

Students who have voice will share it more widely and often. Parents are primarily connected through their child and when they have a clear idea of what is going on, they will be more likely to make contact, come in for meetings and attend events. The students are the key stakeholders in this case, and allowing them a seat at the table is the key to unlocking a whole new potential for connectivity and growth.

When student voice is a prominent component within schools and is supported by policies and programs, students are empowered to engage in their own learning, make suggestions, ask questions and develop proposals (Lac & Cumings Mansfield, 2018; Shier, 2019; Vaughn, 2021). The sharing of this power promotes environments in which students develop essential critical and creative thinking skills, demonstrating to young people that they can be agents of change and "knowledge creators, not just receivers" (Mitra, 2018, p.474).

Look for?

1. Shallow efforts at 'voice'.

Just because a student puts on the uniform and attends, does not mean they feel they are connected or they belong. If most efforts to provide voice to school communities – whether that be students or their parents – are limited in the sharing of perspective or contribution, then they are really community involvement, not community voice.

It is essential that looking for these surface-level events, initiatives or programs becomes a primary focus in our pursuit of connection across a school. I have heard many times from very successful educational leaders that voice starts in the classroom. I have the utmost respect for these leaders and their incredible achievements across their career and I certainly agree with that statement to a degree, but I am much more fearful that most efforts in classrooms are *involvement masquerading as voice* (Hands, 2014).

Choice is not voice. You have provided them options, fantastic, but how have they contributed beyond a participatory role? Focus Area 5 is asking you to look for opportunities for students to be involved from the development level, not just the consumer level. It can start in the classroom, but then needs to go much further. We need a future designed by students, not defined for them.

2. Co-opting of student voice.

Data is often collected from students in high-performing schools regarding attitudes to learning, social environment, teaching quality and resourcing, but how often is this data shared with or presented by the students themselves? I would guess that in your environment, as in many of mine, this data is presented at staff meetings and as the basis for professional learning days.

Schools avoid student voice when it comes to the discussion, planning and facilitation of school improvement (Jones & Bubb, 2021). This is not surprising considering student voice is often characterised by democratic processes, while school improvement is more strongly correlated with "effectiveness and efficiency" (Jones & Bubb, 2021, p.3).

A growing collection of research is concerned with the reduction of authentic student participation and the co-opting of student voice to demonstrate commitment to change (Mitra, 2018; Ralph, 2021). According to Mitra (2018), this is becoming increasingly prevalent as student voice is added to indicators of a successful school under the banner of 'excellence' and utilised for the purposes of school advertising and communication for prospective families.

This 'tokenistic' approach is the antithesis to authentic student voice and merely meets the departmental standards while encouraging little real change (Jones & Bubb, 2021, p.3). Focus Area 5 requires you to look for opportunities to position students as key agents of change in their school.

Decision-making should not be a power struggle or a zero-sum game in education (Gregory & Mebane, 2020). We are all on the same team. Students should know this, feel this and see this in action.

3. If, then reward systems.

Student voice is often squashed by the opinions of the adults in the room (Ralph, 2021). Some students, such as those with lower grades, behavioural concerns and a distinct lack of badges on their uniform, are often ignored completely (Pearce & Wood, 2019).

When considering student voice, *if, then* cannot be a contributing factor when deciding who speaks, who listens or what voices hold value (Jones & Bubb, 2021). Token approaches to student voice are almost exclusively bound to *if, then* reward systems in which students are disempowered to further their learning or extend their abilities, as they are busy reacting to a bribe from an adult.

Students do not have the time or the audience to provide their opinions because if they do not complete the current task, they will need to complete it at recess. But what if the student was given the space to explain their thoughts on the task itself, its rationale, its purpose?

Student voice, and teaching more widely, must be characterised by consistent challenges to engage, and not bribing into compliance (Pink, 2011). All students, despite their experience or history at their school, should have the opportunity to share their expertise and see their contributions reflected in visible action from teachers and leaders (Pearce & Wood, 2019; Ralph, 2021).

Too often, schools are focused on *if, then* and catching students both doing the wrong and, at times, the right thing, to reinforce a point. Focus Area 5 wants you to look for these moments, built on historical teacher-student biases, and see the opportunity for listening to a salient critique of a school policy, rather than purely an argumentative student absorbing precious time.

Which way?

Authentic approaches to student voice shift the power dynamic of a classroom, schoolyard or institution to allow meaningful decisions to be made in collaboration rather than teacher directed. Meaningful initiatives are those that are built on mutual and reciprocal accountability, they are school-wide and framed around reflecting, discussing, generating dialogue and acting (Byker et al., 2017). It is essential then, that we understand that any initiative that primarily focuses on increasing academic achievements or school-wide levels of attainment is not an authentic approach to increasing student voice and should be avoided by policymakers (Cook-Sather, 2018).

Several frameworks have found popularity not only within academic literature but also in practice, and can be utilised when introducing and designing student-voice initiatives. Professor Laura Lundy (2007) designed her model (see Figure 10 below) around four key interrelated components: Space, Voice, Audience and Influence, each required to ensure a student's participation and voice is authentically heard.

Figure 10: Lundy's model of participation

Space	Voice	Audience	Influence
Children must be guaranteed a safe space, where they can feel free to discuss, share, debate and decide what they want to say and how to say it, and plan their actions.	Children must be provided with the support they need to be able to speak out and express their views. They must have access to the right resources to ensure their voice is heard.	Those responsible for the decisions that affect children's lives, concerns and opportunities must be willing to hear what they have to say.	Decision-makers must be willing to accept their obligation to give due weight to children's views, and to take them into account in decisions affecting their lives.

(ADAPTED FROM LUNDY, 2007)

Lundy's model emphasises the need for young people to have a safe and supportive space to share and feel comfortable doing so. They need methods and devices to enable them to share and express their thoughts. They need to be listened to and have the appropriate audience and, once shared, a student's views must be acted upon (Lundy, 2007).

Aiming for simplicity, a second model of note is Gerison Lansdown's model (see Figure 11 below), which summarised student voice into three levels of engagement: Consultation, in which teachers ask students for their views and nothing else; Collaboration, where teachers and students work collaboratively and share responsibility; and Child-led, where initiatives are organised or facilitated by students, either with support or without (Shier, 2019).

Figure 11: Lansdown's model of engagement

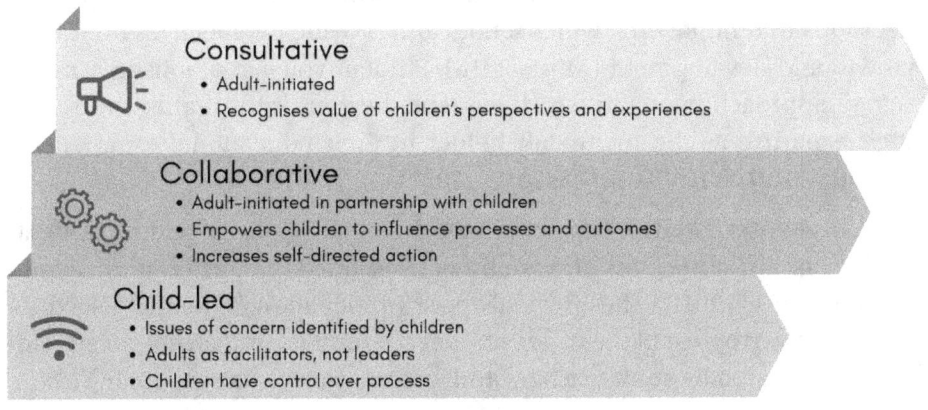

(ADAPTED FROM SHIER, 2019)

Ultimately, the most important component of any model, framework or approach to student voice is empowerment (Shier, 2019). As such, this is the key directional characteristic towards any increase in voice and connection within your school. Much like the models themselves, Lubelfeld et al. (2018) highlights that empowerment needs to be created through a concerted effort to be authentic and effective.

Teachers (and other adults) cannot simply assume they can empower young people. Simply designing and facilitating an enabling environment is not enough on its own, rather, teachers should focus on "the model of conditions, capacities, and attitude/self-belief" that will most likely enable a young person to move towards empowerment and transformation (Shier, 2019, p.5). Students who feel empowered to speak and share within their classroom "develop a role as agents of social change rather than subjects of social control" (Shier, 2019, p.2).

What now?

Developing authentic student voice is essential to sustainable efforts at creating whole-school connection. Within the classroom a shift of the power dynamic allows students to understand the influence of their perspectives, their actions and their effect within the classes in which they participate (Treacy & Leavy, 2021).

The literature highlights that true student voice, however, is not just contained to the classroom environment and involves shifting the power across multiple facets of the school community, allowing students to participate in decisions that impact the wider school and provide perspectives on future growth and development (Mitra, 2018). Student voice in a holistic, whole-school approach is one in which students become consultants and share their expertise as the main stakeholder in their educational experiences (Halliday et al., 2019; Treacy & Leavy, 2021).

Student Representative Councils have been a staple of many student leadership structures within a number of schools in the Western world (Baroutsis et al., 2016). These formal opportunities allow for a small selection of students to represent the wider student community and engage in guided conversation led by adult teachers and leaders (Baroutsis et al., 2016).

While these councils can provide unique opportunities for voice, the environment and the nature of their implementation is aligned with control rather than empowerment, and the nature of these councils is varied depending on contextual politics and the maintenance of traditional school roles (Baroutsis et al., 2016; Fleming, 2015; Gunter & Thomson, 2007).

> In a qualitative study of schools in Norway, Jones and Bubb (2021) conducted focus groups with both students and teachers. One topic analysed was Student Council Membership, a regulated requirement in Norwegian schools. A 13-year-old participant stated:
>
> > "When we give our opinion, teachers say, 'yeah, yeah, we'll do something about it later', and then they never end up doing anything. That makes me feel annoyed. If they are going to use class time to ask us and then not do anything about it, then it's a waste of time. If teachers aren't going to do anything about our opinion, then don't ask us." (p.12)
>
> A lack of structure in this instance created issues leading to students feeling unheard.

Stepping outside of these roles and embracing a change in the council model of student leadership can provide opportunities for students to directly contribute to school improvement, and not only their own individual improvement in the classroom (Charteris & Smardon, 2019). Frameworks must be designed to support the positioning of students as influential in the writing and approving of policy and whole-school improvement agendas (Yuen, 2022). Contemporary schools have far too great a focus on accountability and outcomes (Keddie, 2015), and this exacerbates the critiques of student voice as simply a measure of further control (Yuen, 2022).

Learning environments will continue to support the suppression of student voice and re-establish traditional power relationships unless the adults relinquish their control and accept students as partners in their learning (Charteris & Smardon, 2019; Keddie, 2015). In contexts where student voice is restricted to the classroom and controlled by curriculum standards and mandatory high-stakes assessment, the true voice of the students within a school will be silenced and their ability to reach their full potential and confirm their expertise and position as a valued member of their community will be diminished (Robinson & Taylor, 2013).

Let's go!

Takeaway #1: Students should never feel powerless when it comes to their schooling.

Traditionally, students and teachers have had very specific roles to play within a school (Hands, 2014). These roles may have worked in the past, but it is time to change. We can facilitate and foster an environment that embraces student voice and starts our organisation on the connection journey by relinquishing the power dynamics of traditional school (Cook-Sather, 2020). In a connected school, students and teachers are partners in shared learning experiences.

> **Consider the following:**
> How often are students responsible for actions leading to whole-school change in your school?
> - What is supporting or preventing this from being the reality?

Thinking about your position as a teacher.
- Why does the teacher need to be the dominant voice in the classroom?
- What is one small change you could make to shift the power away from control and towards collaboration?

Takeaway #2: Opportunities for voice should not be shallow or tokenistic.

Young people are incredibly perceptive, and they know when something is genuine and when it is for show (Shier, 2019). Student voice efforts cannot be for marketing or presentation purposes, it must be genuinely for the benefit of the students, the teachers, the leaders and the wider community (Lac & Cumings Mansfield, 2018). Ultimately, this is the key difference between the sausage sizzle and a genuine community feel that is present every single day. Authentic and genuine student voice creates a culture of collaboration, a vibe you can feel on a campus. You want the vibe to remain well after the barbecue is finished.

Consider the following:

Do students feel valued at your school?
- How do you know this?
- Can this evidence (or lack thereof) be used to support positive change towards authentic student voice and sustainable connection?

Does your school currently run events or provide opportunities for students to share their voice?
- Who manages and facilitates these events?
- Could this be changed/improved?

Takeaway #3: Empowerment builds connection.

Empowered students are more engaged and feel greater levels of connection to the world around them (Lubelfeld et al., 2018). Empowering students and providing a platform through student-voice initiatives and activities allows teachers to generate a greater understanding of the social environment, the varied perspectives and learning experiences of different students and the facilitation of a classroom that meets the individual and collective students' needs and expectations (Cook-Sather, 2020; Vaughn, 2021).

Consider the following:

Think about a team/group/partnership you are currently in.

- What actions could you take within your role to facilitate co-creation within your lessons, faculty or team?
- How can the students be involved from the concept stage?
- How could you ensure this was being reflected in other classrooms and by your peers?

What potential professional development would you and your colleagues require to make positive steps towards authentic student voice?

- What would make this more likely to be effective in your context?
- What are the existing barriers that would need to be addressed?

CHAPTER 9
Houston, we have lift-off!
Focus Area 6: Permission

Trust is a key contributor to any connection, whether that be between people, pets or technology. Beyond basic trust lies permission, a superpower for forming authentic connection. Permission recognises a level of established trust that strengthens and sustains connection through times of change. Connected schools require this level of trust to be able to not only manage the dynamic realities of their community, but provide the support for them to flourish.

This chapter explores the concept of permission and its links to growth, health and wellbeing, and leadership. Several rules surrounding permission exist in schools that have stood the test of time, but must be readdressed to create a supportive environment for connection. Discussion of these changes is framed through Hardin's Theory of Trust to create an environment that supports permission that is reciprocal, purposeful and community building.

May I?

From the earliest years of life, we are constantly taught the power behind permission. Permission is an essential component of society; it keeps us in line and ensures that our world as we know it functions in the way we expect it to.

We need to embrace this – nobody is arguing for anarchy here – but embrace it only to a certain point. Because permission is a double-edged sword. It can equally create psychological safety, encourage collaboration and welcome vulnerability, but it can also be restrictive, increase control systems and hinder growth.

While we often think of permission as asking for something, this is incredibly limiting. This chapter is not about using manners or seeking someone's approval, this is about trust: trust in oneself and trust conveyed between an individual and their community.

This is essential, as developing community members who believe in their work is one of the core aims of education, or at least it should be. A community that grants the power to follow and act on those personal beliefs creates a level of trust that is invaluable to the connection journey.

At its core, permission is the gifting or relinquishing of something valuable, whether that be time, attention or perhaps if you are committed to change, power. It is for this reason that permission is so vital to sustainable connection, as mishandling permission leads down a long and arduous road littered with mistrust.

In a school environment, permission serves as an essential component of any sustainable effort for change and the promotion of shared understanding among teachers, students and parents. Permission is an essential Focus Area in this framework as it holds incredible significance when considering the establishment of trust, through effective communication and shared respect, both necessary for connection within a community.

Transforming how we manage permission in schools today is essential for fostering a more inclusive, adaptive and collaborative educational environment. Instead of the traditional top-down approach, schools should look to increase participation, seeking input and permission from teachers, students and parents.

As it currently stands, students are participants, parents are bystanders and teachers are authority, all by design. To shift the nature of connection in our schools we must embrace a new approach to permission, one that is role adverse and allows for all community members to be equal and active contributors, without the need for asking first.

This is not simply I trust you to do something *I want* you to do.

This is I trust you to do what *you think* is right and *I will support* you to do it.

Tell me!

The concept of permission is incredibly important to all of us, but it is vital to young people (Abdelzadeh & Lundberg, 2017; Görlich & Katznelson, 2015). As students attempt to navigate the choppy waters of relationships, permission may dictate how their understanding of the world develops and their fit within it (Griffith, et al., 2018).

Schools that not only grant permission for learner autonomy but also teach skills linked to self-permission, create a safe space for the development of worldly understanding and, as a result, are invaluable for their potential to positively influence each young life (Görlich & Katznelson, 2015; Gregory, 2017; Rashad, 2018). Students who can learn the value of granting self-permission early promote personal growth, positive self-expression and the development of meaningful connections within their community (Gregory, 2017; Mayger & Hochbein, 2021).

Connected schools are ones that empower learners to lead with authenticity and passion. Permission takes on a critical role in developing this type of environment as this type of movement plays antagonist to the traditional structure of education (Ghamrawi et al., 2023).

The traditional academic environment often creates an insurmountable challenge to granting permission, restricted by historical and societal expectations and norms, which speak freedom and agency, but can inadvertently stress conformity (Ghamrawi et al., 2023; Gregory, 2017). If young people can gain the trust to grant themselves permission and autonomy (Banwo et al., 2022), they are liberated to engage in deep and passion-fuelled learning that frees them from predetermined moulds (Fenlon & Fitzgerald, 2021; Görlich & Katznelson, 2015; Rashad, 2018). This is incredibly important as schools look to embrace each unique identity and strive to facilitate an inclusive environment that celebrates the diversity of the school community (Ghamrawi et al., 2023; Ford & Ware, 2018).

Growth cannot be obtained without degrees of permission. Increased student agency and the space to grant self-permission is essential when creating programs that encourage personalised experiences (Holden, 2021) that explore diverse interests, and the pursuit of goals and aspirations (Rashad, 2018).

Encouraging this mindset nurtures a culture of resilience and adaptability, but further creates the fertile ground for an environment where students feel empowered to take risks, learn from their experiences and develop into active members of their communities (Griffith, et al., 2018; Holden, 2021; Mayger & Hochbein, 2021; Woods-Groves et al., 2019).

Outside of academics, permission is critical to the development of mental and emotional wellbeing, both in individuals and towards the development of a positive and supportive school community (Rashad, 2018; Riley, 2019; Tschannen-Moran, 2014). The priorities of education today place an incredible series of challenges at the feet of young people, and students must have the permission to prioritise their mental health, seek support when needed and engage in learning that develops self-care (Ungar et al., 2014).

While the focus remains purely on academics, this will likely not be the result. Connected schools are and will be those that accept and recognise their role in developing resilience and emotional intelligence over traditional metrics of student success (Ford & Ware, 2018; Ungar et al., 2014).

A shift towards true permission will serve as a catalyst for more creative and innovative practice (Tschannen-Moran, 2014). While schools strive to create collaboration, historical notions of power and permission limit the success of these ventures.

One of the last bastions of the resistance to change in education is the structured and tokenistic approach to student expression (Rashad, 2018). Often labelled immature and juvenile, the ideas, perspectives and talents of students are often overlooked or embraced too shallowly.

This drastically reduces the depth at which a community can connect with each other and limits the collaborative power of a school population (Ford & Ware, 2018). Structural change is required to ensure that schools live up to be the vibrant communities they claim to be, providing equal opportunity for all students to thrive, irrespective of their background or identity (Ghamrawi et al., 2023).

The education system must acknowledge and actively challenge the conscious and unconscious biases that govern it, to truly take steps towards the creation of a learning environment that is truly equitable and just (Tschannen-Moran, 2014). Schools that actively work towards societal permission foster a community where every student feels seen, heard and valued (Ford & Ware, 2018; Mayger & Hochbein, 2021).

Schools that embrace and encourage this concept contribute to the holistic development of their students, fostering an environment where individuality is celebrated, connections are strengthened (Mayger & Hochbein, 2021) and everyone can thrive.

Look for?

1. Permission to be a student and only a student.

There are very few other roles in life that are as restrictive as the role of the student; a role that keeps 'good' students in chairs under desks and in rows. Students are taught to raise their hand to speak, to ask to move from their seat or request to attend the bathroom.

While these examples are a little trivial, they are about creating and establishing control. For the most part, students in traditional models of school only have permission to act and speak like a student and nothing greater (Görlich & Katznelson, 2015; Rashad, 2018).

This is reinforced by teachers, parents and by the students themselves through repetitious conditioning every year. In considering any other relationship, power, control and restriction would be dirty, heinous words. In education, they are the norm.

Students need the freedom to explore their space and reconnect the curious parts of their nature. Is there any doubt as to why older students, many years into the control model of schooling, show a lack of imagination or urgency in their learning? Students cannot break the mould themselves; they will need guidance and role modelling along the way (Mayger & Hochbein, 2021).

~~Lead~~
Guide

Focus Area 6 wants you to look for opportunities to do away with classroom rules that govern a student's permission to think, feel and act. Rather focus on empowering students with expectations, goals and practices that restore, not restrict, giving students an environment that supports partnership *with* adults, not participation *for* them.

2. Restrictions based on history.

Education is consistently stuck in a rut. Even the most innovative schools still struggle to move away from the structures of the past and the historically concrete expectations of what an education should look like. There is no space for this kind of organisation in the rapidly approaching future.

We can no longer emphasise and rely on a pattern of action that reflects "that's just the way we do things here, we always have". Schools scream growth, but fail to give themselves permission to change their ways and the flexibility to support those changes. Large-scale, community-level change is what is required and, make no mistake, it is incredibly difficult and time-consuming. However, this need not be a disheartening statement.

Across the world, young people are voicing their needs and making their thoughts known on all matter of topics, education being just one of them. The impetus for change has been – and is being – created by the students themselves; we, as educators, need only grant the permission required to start acting on it.

Greater individualisation and greater flexibility can be achieved if students are granted permission to shape their learning, teachers are granted permission to escape the recycled unit plans and parents are granted permission to ask questions, be heard and be involved to the level they feel comfortable with (Sun et al., 2023; Strier & Katz, 2016).

Focus Area 6 wants you to look for opportunities to discard the rollover from last year and co-create something new with members of the community. Many hands make light work – they just need to know they can.

3. Yes, but only if...

It should be noted that some students, parents and teachers do have more permission or at least certain degrees of autonomy within traditional schools. Unfortunately, these allowances generally close more doors than they open.

Leadership positions for students, positions of responsibility for teachers and parent positions on school councils are some of these examples. With these come an increase in permission, certainly more so than typical community members, but many of these positions are underutilised, linked to tradition and do not amount to any significant impact on the wider school population.

When we limit permission in these ways we send a stark message to the remaining community, albeit unintentionally perhaps, that with time-served, or a badge or a title comes trust (Gregory, 2017). Trust you should aspire to. A seat closer to the head of the table. A change from normal duties, with increased expectations and rewards. All of it is based on control, very little of it is genuine and, therefore, it certainly has an impact on connection, but not the kind we are after.

Yes, but only if you hold this level, position or influence is not sustainable and not how sustainable connection is formed. Permission cannot be based on a caveat. If anything, the conditions to be met are someone in your community is asking a question, and we should work together to find out or, at the very least, let them explore it themselves (Ghamrawi et al., 2023).

Focus Area 6 wants you to look for the provisos that traditional education has embedded in its foundation: the small, seemingly insignificant things that restrict our schools from being truly open and collaborative.

Things like the opinions of the parent with the larger wallet holding more value.

Things like the college captain having more say than the student with the least interest in leadership.

Things like the teacher who has been on staff the longest holding court while the quieter, newer and more innovative staff member sits quietly.

No more buts.

Which way?

When considering permission, reciprocity is the ultimate goal. A connected community is one that sees the value of each member's potential contribution and aligns this with the work required to develop high-quality learning experiences for students, an enriching workplace for staff, and a supportive and trusting environment for parents (Strier & Katz, 2016; Sun et al., 2023).

Hardin's (2002) Theory of Trust subtly differentiates between one-sided and two-sided trust, which aligns well within the context of connection and all its intricacies and complexities (Keren, 2020). In schools, Hardin's theory is particularly appropriate as teachers navigate the delicate balance of extending permission to their students while fostering an environment that encourages reciprocal trust.

Initially, how permission and trust must be developed in education aligns closely with the concept of one-sided trust (see Figure 12 opposite). This is where administrators or teachers demonstrate consistency through the establishment of norms and the role-modelling of high-impact learning strategies establishing classrooms (and by extension schools) that create security for self-expression, inquiry and active participation in the life of the community, whether that be within the classroom or otherwise. Permission in this manner is extended unilaterally, creating the foundation for a mutually trusting educational environment (Cook & Santana, 2020; Keren, 2020).

Figure 12: One-sided trust

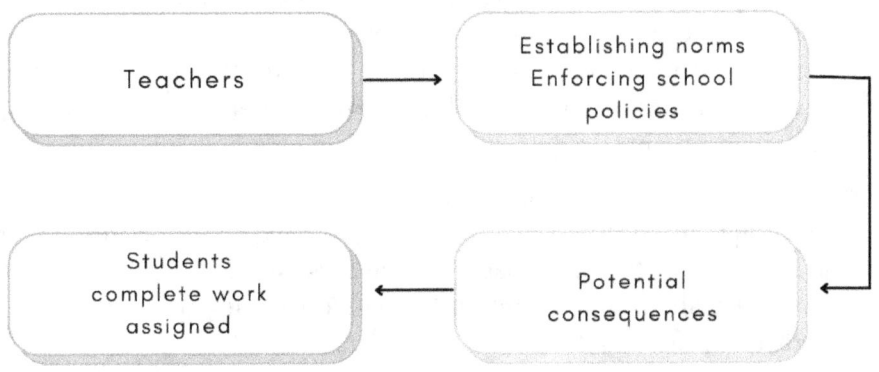

(ADAPTED FROM HARDIN, 2002)

In traditional schooling, a one-sided relationship is typically the end of the road. In a connected school, the journey must progress, it must evolve into a two-sided dynamic (see Figure 13 below). The modelling of this reciprocity becomes critical to the success along the connection journey in an educational organisation, as educators, parents and students learn to trust each other equally.

Educators, by consistently demonstrating integrity, reliability and a genuine commitment to the success and wellbeing of the students in their care, create an environment where students (and by extension their parents) feel comfortable reciprocating the same trust (Cook & Santana, 2020). This reciprocal trust becomes a cornerstone of the connective experience, developing an environment in which all community members have the permission to engage authentically in the life of the school.

Figure 13: Two-sided trust

(ADAPTED FROM HARDIN, 2002)

When young people feel they are working within an environment founded in trust, they are more likely to grant themselves permission to explore, experiment and be more creative in their learning (Rashad, 2018). Teachers are more likely to actively participate in the life of the wider school community, sharing ideas and contributing to an authentically collaborative learning environment (Holden, 2021).

Permission, through the lens of Hardin's theory, is much more than access to educational resources, materials or tangible experiences. Permission at this level allows the safe space for teachers, students and parents to embrace vulnerability and, therefore, increase the clarity, commitment and connectivity throughout the learning process.

In order to embrace a change from the traditional model of schooling, permission, as the basis for trust within a school community, must be embedded in the leadership culture (Mayger & Hochbein, 2021). Principals must embrace their responsibility to create environments where educators, students and their parents have permission to actively engage in the learning process (Ghamrawi et al., 2023).

If this can be cultivated, school leaders create an environment where permission is automatically granted for the creation of innovative practice, organisational changes and collaborative initiatives that contribute to the continual improvement of the educational experience (Ghamrawi et al., 2023) and the creation of sustainable connection.

What now?

Permission is inherently linked to power. Young people have a far greater capacity for responsibility, ownership and control than we give them credit for. Traditional power dynamics in schools need to be disposed of and we desperately need to shift whole schools towards the modelling of trust made tangible through the granting of permission, more often and more widely (Mayger & Hochbein, 2021).

Think of a teacher. Permission from leadership to run their class in a style that fits to their personality and strengths may be the key to developing a cohesive and effective learning environment. This sense of freedom (and I really mean sense) allows the teacher to work at their best as they feel invested in the process (Tschannen-Moran, 2014). Too much of this freedom and in the wrong hands, however, may have the opposite effect and be detrimental to the student experience.

The key is permission with ongoing support. Autonomy does not mean flying solo at all points and ad infinitum. Leaders must start small, build trust and gradually introduce more autonomy (Ghamrawi et al., 2023) and permission for staff to use it.

Permission Also permission

You don't have to go it alone
(but you can)

For teachers, the granting of permission is so vital to maintaining an effective, balanced and connected classroom dynamic. When a teacher feels they have the trust to act in the best interests of their space, it spreads the power and grants the teacher personal ownership over their practice (Banwo et al., 2022).

When a teacher feels this level of empowerment, they are more likely to seek and grant permission within the classroom, engaging students in learning that is inclusive, personal and autonomous (Banwo et al., 2022; Ghamrawi et al., 2023).

When young people enter a school where they believe their opinions are respected and their choices explored, they are more inclined to be an active contributor to discussions and collaborative tasks, and to feel a sense of ownership over their learning (Mayger & Hochbein, 2021). Again, granting this sense of autonomy enhances the classroom dynamic and nurtures the relationships required for progression on the connection journey.

Students who feel valued are much more likely to feel as though they belong (Riley, 2019). When provided the opportunity to grant or deny permission, a student is encouraged to think critically, developing crucial decision-making skills.

These skills are essential to preparation for post-school responsibilities and the unknown challenges they will face in the workforce of the future (Fenlon & Fitzgerald, 2021). Core competencies such as reflection, interpreting feedback, respecting boundaries and understanding the consequences of actions are directly linked to increased student permission (Woods-Groves et al., 2019).

When this is coupled with the solidification of parents as active stakeholders in a young person's learning (Sun et al., 2023), through open communication outside of reporting time or where traditional consent for activities is required increases the holistic development of the student, and validates a parent's position as the primary support for their child. Approaching from this collaborative direction creates fertile ground for connection, community and three-way shared responsibility for the wellbeing and success of the students.

If schools (and preferably systems) can engage in this change earnestly, it will empower students to re-engage with their learning. With increased permission, teachers will feel less restrained, freer and therefore able to cater to diversified needs in the manner they know is best for the students in their individual classrooms. In addition, parental-school relationships will be stronger and more engaging, as parents feel active in their support role, contributing to the holistic education every school website delights in.

Let's go!

Takeaway #1: Permission is given purposefully.

Throughout this chapter there has been significant discussion about giving a greater level of permission and modelling trust within our communities. It is essential this is given, but it is given purposefully.

Do not assume you have given permission or that a student, parent or teacher has received it because you intended it to be so. It is essential that permission that engages the connection journey, that builds community autonomy is given openly and directly. If in doubt, check. Give it purposefully and it will mean more, no matter who the recipient is.

> **Consider the following:**
> What opportunities exist currently where you could grant a little more autonomy?
> - Outside of any child-safe or protective policies, what is your most restrictive policy?
> - Is it possible that this could be amended to create more freedom?
>
> How can you grant permission to your parent community so that they may feel connected and an active contributor to their child's learning?
> - What methods have you tried in the past? Why did they fail/succeed?

Takeaway #2: Permission is essential for learning in the 21st century.

For a school community to be able to freely share and explore their ideas and then conduct any form of work and action towards positive organisational change, they must have permission to do so from school leaders.

Permission is a simple thing to be provided to students, but it is often not, despite its transformative power particularly in critical and creative thinking skill development. The workforce needs of the future are constantly in flux, but these skills will forever be required (Fenlon & Fitzgerald, 2021). Permission and trust create the empowered environment where these skills flourish.

> **Consider the following:**
> Looking through your school's current planning and marketing materials, how significant is the notion of 21st-century skill-building?
> - Do you believe your current methods are achieving the goals outlined?
>
> In what contexts might introducing increased autonomy for students be difficult?
> - What are the barriers?
> - With those known, can you remove them?

Takeaway #3: Permission demonstrates trust, trust builds community.

Permission is the tangible manifestation of trust. When you give a community the permission to ask, explore and engage, you create an environment that is innately conducive to learning (Ghamrawi et al., 2023). Small acts of trust sow the seeds for greater connection gains in the future. Top-down, authoritarian models do not build community, they build conformity.

> **Consider the following:**
>
> How can you bring your community into the school on a regular basis?
>
> - How might the skills, talents and knowledge of your community be leveraged for positive change and growth?
>
> What is the smallest change you could make to increase teacher and learner autonomy from a leadership perspective?
>
> - What are the potential gains from this change?
> - What are the threats?
> - What have you got to lose?

PART 3
SUSTAINING CONNECTION

"People leave traces of themselves where they feel most comfortable, most worthwhile"

HARUKI MURAKAMI

Change is difficult. Organisational change is even more so (Ford et al., 2021).

Part 3: Sustaining connection aims to address the question: *Where do we go from here?* This may be one of the most important questions in the book. I have experienced a lot of initiatives that have started strong and then disappeared into the ether. We cannot let that continue to occur regarding connection.

Motivating and sustaining change in this space will require strength, bravery and buy-in. As Ford et al. (2021) states, it is important not to declare success too early, switch focus or lose constancy of purpose. Avoid a reversion to the status quo by being clear on where you want to be and how you will attempt the journey.

The final chapter of this book, Chapter 10, aims to address this by clarifying sustainability, which like connection, is a muddied concept at best. It also provides you with some last notes on the entirety of The Connection Curriculum, with the focus on building a strong argument for change, whether that is for leadership, teachers, parents, students or yourself, using one of my favourite tools for prioritisation and goal setting, the Eisenhower Matrix, to help you get going.

CHAPTER 10
Making it all work

Sustainable school-wide connection requires the juggling of multiple components from the students, parents and staff that make up your community to the work suggested by the dimensions and Focus Areas in Part 2. One of the last considerations is *how*. Not only, how do you approach this level of organisational change, but how do you propose change at this scale to directors, principal teams, teachers, parents and the students?

This chapter begins with some clarifications on the concept of sustainability before delving into a guide to help you build your case for connection in your context. Utilising President Dwight Eisenhower's Matrix to prioritise tasks, projects and initiatives, this chapter aims to give you the tools, the provocations and the motivation to go forth and engage your community in the work that will see them progress along the connection journey, creating a true community of learning and shared experience.

A note on sustainability

I wish we all understood sustainability a little bit better. In 1987, the United Nations Brundtland Commission (1987) made it pretty clear in my opinion:

> "Meeting the needs of the present without compromising the ability of future generations to meet their own needs."

Near the beginning of the book, I stated schools need to shift away from constantly looking to the past or too far into the future while embarking on the connection journey. I suggested history is not created by solely looking into the past or having your focus too far into the unknowns of the future. You create positive change by pushing forward with courage in the moment. Here, towards the end of the book, we can take this further.

Sustainability is essentially all about coexistence. The biggest differences between the whole planet and your school community are scale and context. The concept is the same at its core: provide for your community now, without it coming at the detriment of the future (Bellei et al., 2020). Seems simple enough in writing, but schools have a terrible track record of keeping things simple.

Sustainable change in schools is a genuine issue because schools have become so unfocused in their aims. They are either looking to create change for now *or* create change for the future, but very seldom are they designing and implementing approaches that would effectively do both (Bellei et al., 2020).

Key to making considerable change to this current state is to redefine what it means to sustain something. Schools and school leaders struggle with sustainable change because they view sustainability as an outcome. A goal. This is, and cannot be, the case. Sustainable change is a process much more ambitious than simply maintenance (DuPuis & Ball, 2013). Consider the following definition:

> "Sustainability does not simply mean whether something will last. It also addresses how particular initiatives can be developed without compromising the development of others in the surrounding environment now and in the future" (Hargreaves & Fink, 2004, p.30).

This definition from Hargreaves and Fink opens the door to innovation and dispels any notion of stagnation or equilibrium. Sustainable change is a process, sustainable connection is a journey. There is no treading water here. The current is too strong. You will lose all your ground gained if you hesitate, or sink to the bottom if you pause for too long.

For the concepts in The Connection Curriculum to have any tangible benefit, we need to understand that connection is a commitment and one that will require ongoing and substantial attention to experience success (DuPuis & Ball, 2013). Like the community of your school, the variables will constantly be changing, and your plans, goals and needs connection-wise will be required to change with them.

While you can consider connecting your school community as an outcome, I would encourage you to see it as a process that continues infinitely. That's a scary thought perhaps, but it's a realistic one. Sustainability never ends and community connection is bound by the same set of rules (Field, 2016). Individual relationships can end, but a school that constantly strives to build relationships, belonging and meaning within its community, that could be endless.

Building a case for connection

Schools have lots of red tape to navigate when committing to something new and especially something long term. Should you need to present the legitimacy of embarking on your own connection journey as a community to a leadership team, school council or a board of administrators or directors, my hope is that what is detailed in the following sections of this chapter will help you to be convincing and constructive.

An effective process towards sustainability requires a solid structure and foundation to ensure its longevity. While I cannot ensure that the human aspects of your change process will always 'stick to the plan', I can certainly provide the structural inspiration for you to start.

It is my hope that the models and tools described briefly in each of the Focus Areas is valuable in framing your thinking towards the connection journey. Utilising simple and practical tools is certainly my favoured approach when introducing and implementing complex change in a school environment, and I hope to finish strong here.

Sustainable connection requires alignment, adaptability and autonomy to empower everyone in your community so they may be active contributors. Within your school, as it embarks on the connection journey, a mix of contextual and unique challenges and opportunities will appear and need to be managed. Some of these you might be able to predict, some perhaps not, but what you do need to be wary of is much more covert: the gravitational pull of the busywork that consumes leaders, teachers and school staff.

The busywork that destroys change at its roots.

This busywork can absorb so unsympathetically, because schools are notoriously bad at prioritising anything that does not demonstrate immediate gain. This results in leaders and teachers spending much of their time focusing on administration and assessment, and less on what matters most – the change!

While many of these jobs must be done and are likely not going to disappear any time soon, the focus must be on not only what *needs* to be done, but also *how best to work through it*. Regarding connection, where most of the progression is experienced over time rather than seen immediately, staff buy-in may require some structured effort to sell the dream.

Enter the Matrix

The Eisenhower Matrix, a renowned productivity tool for more than 50 years, is perfect for framing your initial steps towards sustainable change and the first steps on a renewed connection journey. It should, if organised well, help you keep the busywork at bay and keep the school running while you initiate your journey to connection.

Figure 14: The Eisenhower Matrix

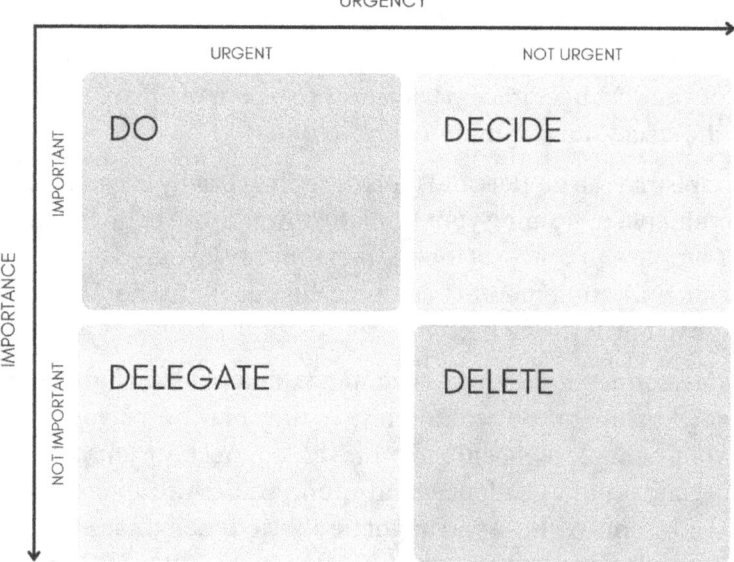

(ADAPTED FROM HILLEN & NEVINS, 2019)

If unfamiliar, the Eisenhower Matrix (see Figure 14 opposite) was designed by Dwight Eisenhower, who was the 34th President of the United States and also a productivity dynamo (Hillen & Nevins, 2019). His methods of juggling multiple high-ranking roles and responsibilities effectively have been extensively studied, and the most utilised, or famous (if that is the right term), is his Matrix. Eisenhower's strategy assists with prioritising tasks based on the following four quadrants:

1. Urgent and important (tasks that need to be completed immediately)
2. Important, but not urgent (tasks that you can schedule for later)
3. Urgent, but not important (tasks you can hand to other people)
4. Neither urgent nor important (tasks that you will maintain or completely remove) (Hillen & Nevins, 2019)

While the matrix, being renowned, could certainly be used as is, to keep to specificity and to frame as much of the focus around connection as possible, I have slightly modified Hillen and Nevins' (2019) version of the matrix (see Figure 15 below) to specifically align with work in the connection space. While each of the quadrants is similar, the variable labelled *important* has become *connection* to specifically frame your thinking around the journey. Let's briefly explore each quadrant.

Figure 15: Modified Eisenhower Matrix

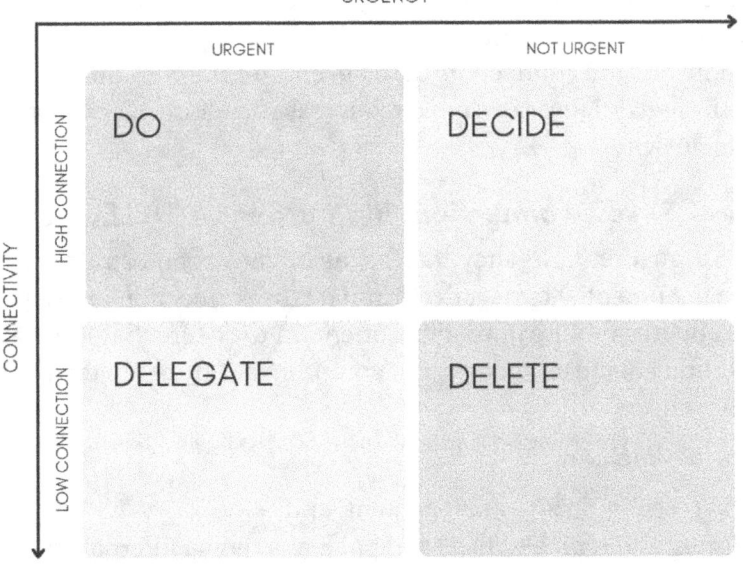

(ADAPTED FROM HILLEN & NEVINS, 2019)

Quadrant 1: High connection, high urgency (DO).

In the first quadrant, initiatives and strategies that require immediate attention based on their high impact on school connection are of the highest priority. In starting the connection journey, despite where that starting point may be, these tasks are essential and must be started immediately to ensure the strongest possible foundation is supporting all future efforts.

Examples may include:

- Creating mentor, coaching and leadership opportunities;
- Planning events and implementing community-building activities; and
- Designing and maintaining channels for open communication among students, teachers and parents.

Quadrant 2: High connection, low urgency (DECIDE).

In the second quadrant, the need to be strategic will be essential as the initiative and strategies in this space yield high impact for connection, but do not have the immediate deadline. These tasks align with longer-term initiatives that sow the seeds of deep and meaningful connection, keeping the community engaged for longer periods of time and contributing to sustainability in both effort and payoff.

Examples may include:

- Professional development planning, specifically long-term, collaborative programs;
- Relationship and connection-based events for the community; and
- Student-led initiatives designed to increase a culture of positivity and inclusivity.

Quadrant 3: Low connection, high urgency (DELEGATE).

In the third quadrant, urgency returns, as initiatives and strategies sitting here have the potential to negatively impact the connection journey. These types of concerns require immediate attention to ensure they are managed efficiently and effectively, and do not compromise any completed or future connection efforts.

Examples may include:

- Conflict resolution and management; and
- Communication breakdowns and policies to guide internal and external communications.

Quadrant 4: Low connection, low urgency (DELETE).

In the final quadrant, initiatives and strategies here do not require immediate attention from a connection perspective, as they are likely to be associated with administration of the school or related process or policy. They are essential to the running of the school* and so cannot technically be 'deleted'; however, their yield connection-wise may be low overall.

Examples may include:

- Daily administration, organisation and processes required to manage the school.

Utilising the Eisenhower Matrix, schools can align tasks with the impact on connection and the urgency in which they should be addressed. This allows for navigating the complexities of the connection journey without compromising or adding incredible burden to the routine school administration.

Sticking to a framework such as this will assist to create an environment that reflects high-quality education in the most traditional sense, but also, more importantly, a thriving network in which meaningful connections create vibrant and inclusive spaces for that learning to take place.

Bringing the focus back

It is my hope that you can identify some overlap and similarities across all the aspects of this book. I hope that this has been conveyed without becoming repetitious. Connection is a web and, as such, addressing connection involves following the pattern of the web, and disseminating the detail at the points where it diverges and equally where it converges.

All six of the Focus Areas rely heavily on one another, hence why there is overlap. In my opinion, overlap is your friend, especially in circumstances where focusing on one area is all your team can manage initially. The interrelatedness of the entire curriculum allows you to focus on one at a time, yet still progress across many of the other five by association, even when this is not your particular focus or where your attention lies.

---

* It is important to note that efficient and effective management of tasks in this quadrant, while low on impact directly, will allow for the allocation of time and resources required to create greater impact across the three other quadrants. A school still needs to be a school!

For this reason, embarking on the connection journey should not be an exercise in keeping a toy in the box it came in. Mix and match. Remove the boundaries between the Focus Areas and seek out the crossover as you are planning, implementing and reviewing. Celebrate each gain successfully made, despite the intentionality of it. No journey worth taking is mapped out perfectly; some of the best additions to it will be the unexpected ones.

The celebration of all gains made on the journey is essential as the shift towards sustainable connection will be guarded by perception, caution and scepticism. Whether this is presented by a parent, a colleague or a student, we must not be dismayed. Intent to connect is not enough to make connection occur. You will need to fight through the barriers.

To authentically connect with those around us, we must take stock of the current climate and plan a slow and methodical journey to success, rather than a rush for the finish line. This will minimise the barriers encountered and increase the chances of success. As such, Matrix in hand, we return to the Focus Areas of The Connection Curriculum and some rousing final remarks for each.

1. Build a new narrative of connection.

How your school reconciles with its organisational identity, and by extension its vision, values and image, is intricate, historical, but also inherently coupled to connection. A strong sense of identity across the school establishes a foundation for genuine connection to flourish, providing students, teachers and parents an environment that represents more than four walls and a whiteboard, but a collective. When a school can instil a sense of identity throughout its community, the individuals within recognise their school's identity is not just a logo or a motto - it is the *people* who belong to it.

> **Consider the following:**
> Re/define core values and mission:
> - Clearly define and articulate the school's core values and mission. Ensure that these statements resonate with the entire school community and provide a foundation for the school's identity.
>
> Engage community members:
> - Involve all stakeholders, including students, parents, teachers and staff, in the development of the school's identity through surveys, workshops or focus groups to ensure a collective understanding and ownership.

Showcase achievements and success stories:
- Regularly celebrate the achievements and success stories of students, teachers and the school community.

2. Light a new pathway towards purpose.

Purpose has long been an intrinsic component of the education experience. The methods in which we establish a sense of purpose in our students, however, need to change. When a school community is embedded with strong relationships and a sense of belonging, communities of support are created, providing the fertile ground for shared exploration of purpose, and meaning beyond careers, income or grades. Purpose-driven education, that which illuminates an individual's why, is not based on a knowledge point or curriculum standard, but becomes a part of the cultural tapestry that embodies the life of the community and the connections within.

Consider the following:

Connect learning to the real world:
- Incorporate real-world examples, projects and community service opportunities that demonstrate the relevance and importance of what they are learning.

Host purposeful events:
- Organise events and activities that reinforce the school's purpose. This could include guest speakers, workshops and seminars that inspire and motivate the community.

Emphasise social and emotional learning:
- Integrate social and emotional learning (SEL) into the curriculum to help students develop a deeper understanding of themselves and their place in the world, fostering a sense of purpose.

3. Create creative creations, creatively.

To be creative is to connect with the people around you. This connection is fundamentally linked with collaboration, exploration and freedom. All forms of creativity, whether they be structured or disruptive, are reliant on being able to freely share ideas and celebrate perspective. Creativity is to be nurtured or it is lost. A connected school prioritises the relationships between individuals, creating the space for innovative thinking, belonging and meaning. In a truly connected school community, creativity paves the pathway to interdisciplinary learning and inspires the leaders of the future.

Consider the following:

Support divergent thinking:
- Asking open-ended questions and promoting multiple perspectives creates an atmosphere where there's no 'wrong' answer, fostering a willingness to take creative risks.

Encourage risk-taking:
- Create an environment where taking risks and making mistakes are viewed as part of the creative process.

Provide time for reflection:
- Build in time for reflection in the curriculum to think deeply about creative processes and learn from experiences.

4. Be guided by the curious heart.

Empathic curiosity is what draws us to the people around us. When connections are being formed, empathic curiosity plays the dual role of the predecessor and the successor. Relationships, and in turn belonging and meaning, fuel empathic curiosity, creating environments characterised by compassion, understanding and shared experience. These skills are not just taught in the classroom, but form the cultural backbone of the community, driving an inclusive and supportive environment that stretches far beyond the classroom.

Consider the following:

Promote diversity and inclusion:
- Teach community members about different cultures, backgrounds and perspectives to broaden their understanding and empathy.

Implement restorative practices:
- Use restorative practices to address conflicts and disciplinary issues to understand the impact of actions and repairing harm, promoting empathy and accountability.

Teach perspective-taking:
- Integrate activities that teach students to see situations from different perspectives.

5. Embrace the voices.

A community that shares its voice is one that is striving to create psychological safety. The voice of students, parents and classroom teachers is often stifled, or worse, tokenistic, and disingenuous in its approach, leading to environments that are impersonal and disconnected. Creating a safe space for communities to share is an essential component of building strong, resilient relationships that increase belonging, and the space for the generation of shared meaning. A culture of shared voices is one that amplifies and champions individuals, providing them the space to actively shape their educational experience.

Consider the following:

Student-led initiatives:

- This could include clubs, projects or events initiated and organised by students with the goal of making a positive impact on the school community.

Collaborative decision-making:

- Include students, teachers and parents in collaborative decision-making processes, such as curriculum development, school policies and extracurricular activities.

Leadership training programs:

- Implement leadership training programs that empower students to develop effective communication skills, confidence and the ability to advocate for themselves and others.

6. Permit exploration, without limits.

Often overlooked or misunderstood, the concept of permission is essential to the connection journey. Permission is reflected by trust and is the by-product of an environment in which autonomous exploration and innovation are encouraged. Strong relationships between individuals create the space for permission to flourish, leading to discovery, experimentation and the extension of learning beyond that mapped in the subject curriculum. Permission, and by extension, trust, map learning experiences to real-world self-management, granting permission to take risks, learn from mistakes and then develop a growth mindset.

Consider the following:

Innovation labs or spaces:

- Create designated spaces within the school where students and teachers can explore new ideas, collaborate on projects, and experiment with different tools and technologies.

Professional development opportunities:

- Offer professional development opportunities that focus on leadership, innovation and permission to equip teachers and staff with the skills and mindset needed to take risks and explore new approaches.

Permission slip for innovation:

- Symbolically introduce a 'permission slip for innovation' to emphasise the importance of giving oneself permission to think creatively and take risks.

The journey is messy

In *Let Go: It's Time for us to let go of Shame, Expectation and our Addiction to Social Media*, Hugh van Cuylenburg (2021) discusses the imperfect nature of human connection. In fact, he states that being imperfect is essentially a requirement. Our flaws, whether we address them directly or not, draw us closer together because they demonstrate vulnerability – usually something we all keep so close to the chest.

The connection journey and its Landmarks of *relationships*, *belonging* and *meaning* is an exercise in vulnerability. Opening yourself to a community of people, who in turn, hopefully, will reciprocate creating stronger and deeper bonds. They are also an exercise in persistence, another quality that holds considerable value to connection.

We need persistence to work with our community to align with identity and purpose, to adapt via creativity and empathic curiosity, and establish autonomy through voice and permission. If we can, we push through the barriers that typically end this process at Landmark 1 and extend the scope of our connectivity. Taking the brilliant, caring and life-changing relationships those in schools create daily, and expanding on them to establish belonging and a culture of shared meaning.

The key, as Van Cuylenburg highlights, is to stop trying to get the journey perfect and just try to get it moving. Your efforts to drive connection alone will lead to the formation of connections. And if worse comes to worst, failure in itself is a platform for connection (Van Cuylenburg, 2021).

Consider this: we often do not know why everything worked or remember much of the detail when something goes perfectly, but we always remember the imperfect days, the struggles and the challenges. We especially remember when they bring us closer together with others and, of course, when there is a laugh or two involved.

Students won't remember the details of your consistently awesome lessons, but they will remember the feeling of walking into your classroom. We want to amplify this contextual gold mine and make it school-wide.

Connection is the goal, but the journey is muddy. If you are coming out clean, you are likely not building sustainable connection. It is the kind that will fade, like those perfect lessons, days and moments.

It is a journey, do not be afraid to explore and, most of all, keep it messy.

Conclusion

Connection is an essential, not a desirable

At the beginning of this book, I shared my frustration with the inflexibility of the education system. It can be very maddening to work within the restrictions of four metaphorical walls when a brighter, more relevant world can be seen outside the window. One solution to this state, not the only solution I must preface, is a focus on connection.

Our ability to connect with those around us is a core part of what makes us human and, as such, we need to make sure we get it right. Connection is essential, and it will continue to be essential whether the messages within this book land or otherwise. While there is vigorous debate about artificial intelligence, automation and jobs being dissolved, lost and modified, all these real-world concerns are not going to remove our need to embrace the humans in our communities. In many regards, they may make it more vital that we are connected.

So, why are we so poorly addressing it? Perhaps it is perspective. I believe that most schools would desire whole-school connectivity, and as discussed earlier in this book, it is likely somewhere in your values, mission, strategic plan or implementation plan, but it is as a desirable, not an essential.

A common theme throughout the Focus Areas discussed in this book is prioritisation. Each of the six Focus Areas are written based on an existing component of contemporary schools; whether they are being planned, actioned or ignored, they are there somewhere. But not as an antecedent to many of the other goals aligned with achievement, wellbeing or engagement.

Connection is not quite an afterthought, but it certainly is not a prominent one. One of the aims of this book is to give you the motivation and suggest some tools to help you act, but to also reframe connection from desirable to intrinsically beneficial to every other goal you are trying to meet in the coming year.

I do not anticipate this book will create widespread change that ends the pursuit of academic achievement as the number one priority of education. But if your understanding of connection has grown while reading, you will know that connection can help the humans *and* the scores, and at the very least it is time for schools to stop being so blind to all the conditions that create an increase in academic excellence (if that is indeed what you are pursuing).

Connected students will work for themselves and be engaged in their learning. They will have a relationship with not only their peers or their teachers, but the school they attend and, most importantly, a positive and long-lasting relationship with *learning*. They will develop a sense of belonging if the environment supports it, creating a psychologically safe space for growth and expression that will increase the meaning of their future pursuits. This will drive their learning to be contextual, interesting, investing and community focused.

Imagine learning that extended from the overpriced, overinflated, oversaturated textbooks and into the real world. Beyond this, students will feel connected to a sense of meaning in their life. They may not have all the pieces in place, but they will feel as though they have a role to play in the future. They will feel as though they are not simply a passive participant or, as my students would say, an NPC (non-playable character), but an active contributor.

Make connection an essential and you will undoubtedly see your grades go up. Continue to focus on the desired result and not the components that take you there and schools will continue to drop in quality and our young people will continue to be punished for our lack of action. It is imperative we make work towards connection more important than a final year score. The ability to take on a new connection journey opens hundreds of potential doors in the future. A final Year 12 score opens one briefly. Are we really going to continue to focus on the smallest, most insignificant and unimportant door over the many?

> In *Ten Survival Skills for a World in Flux*, Tom Fletcher (2022) quotes Charles Darwin, who stated:
>
> > "It's not the strongest of the species who survive, nor the most intelligent, but the one most responsive to change."

The Connection Curriculum is about responding to the needs of our young people by genuinely opening our schools to every member of your community to leverage their potential to contribute their strengths, their histories and their extensive experiential knowledge. We are living in a world where the concept of connection has expanded exponentially through the digitisation of the human experience, but we must not forget that the experience should be unequivocally *human*.

Will somebody think of the children?

Growing up, I loved *The Simpsons* and have found on repeat viewings that the cartoon comedy has several lessons regarding connection, and often these are linked to misunderstandings in perspective. In a great episode, the son, Bart, breaks a gargoyle on a 'witch's' house and as punishment is required to work for the owner. He is surprised to find she is not a witch, and the house is a burlesque house. When his mother, Marge, finds out, she starts a community movement to shut the business down.

The episode is a consistent clash between perspectives, assumptions and panic, culminating in a confrontation between the community and the business owner and her employees. The Reverend's wife, while standing among the outraged community, states: "Won't somebody think of the children?"

Schools, like the concerned Springfield community, should be chiefly concerned with their young people. But in the case of the Reverend's wife, and the case of education today, the concern and the resulting exclamation is made on behalf of the children, without their consultation. I am not advocating for the opposite in the case of this episode, but the perspective of the children was not considered, and the adults came out, torches, pitchforks and all, to defend what they thought their best interests were.

The community rallied without understanding the people within, and schools do much the same thing. Parents are not connected, so they often feel distant and out of the loop. Teachers are feeling overworked and overlooked, some becoming burnt out and reducing the energy available for connection. Students are unheard and undervalued, frustrated with a system that does not support their needs.

We have a chance here to change the way we communicate and to create a partnership of understanding between all as equals. When connection is a priority, we can strengthen our relationships, create a sense of belongingness and form an understanding of meaning in our lives. When it comes to the connection journey, no matter who the member of the community is, we should be asking them, not speaking for them.

A final thought

> **"Alone we can do so little; together we can do so much"**
>
> **HELEN KELLER**

Keller's inspirational quote is a proposition that everyone in your community should identify with in some capacity. Keller, a remarkable woman, identified the strength of looking beyond the small changes that we can create as individuals, and towards community-based change on a larger scale, with a much larger impact.

I truly believe that if your community is exposed to genuine, sustainable connection, the individuals within will change the world. They will have seen it, embraced it and been partner to it. We must come together to embark on the connection journey in any true capacity. The future of the world is reliant on social capital, so invest in the riches you are surrounded with and be rewarded by the returns it will provide.

Bon voyage.

Figure 16: The Connection Curriculum revisited

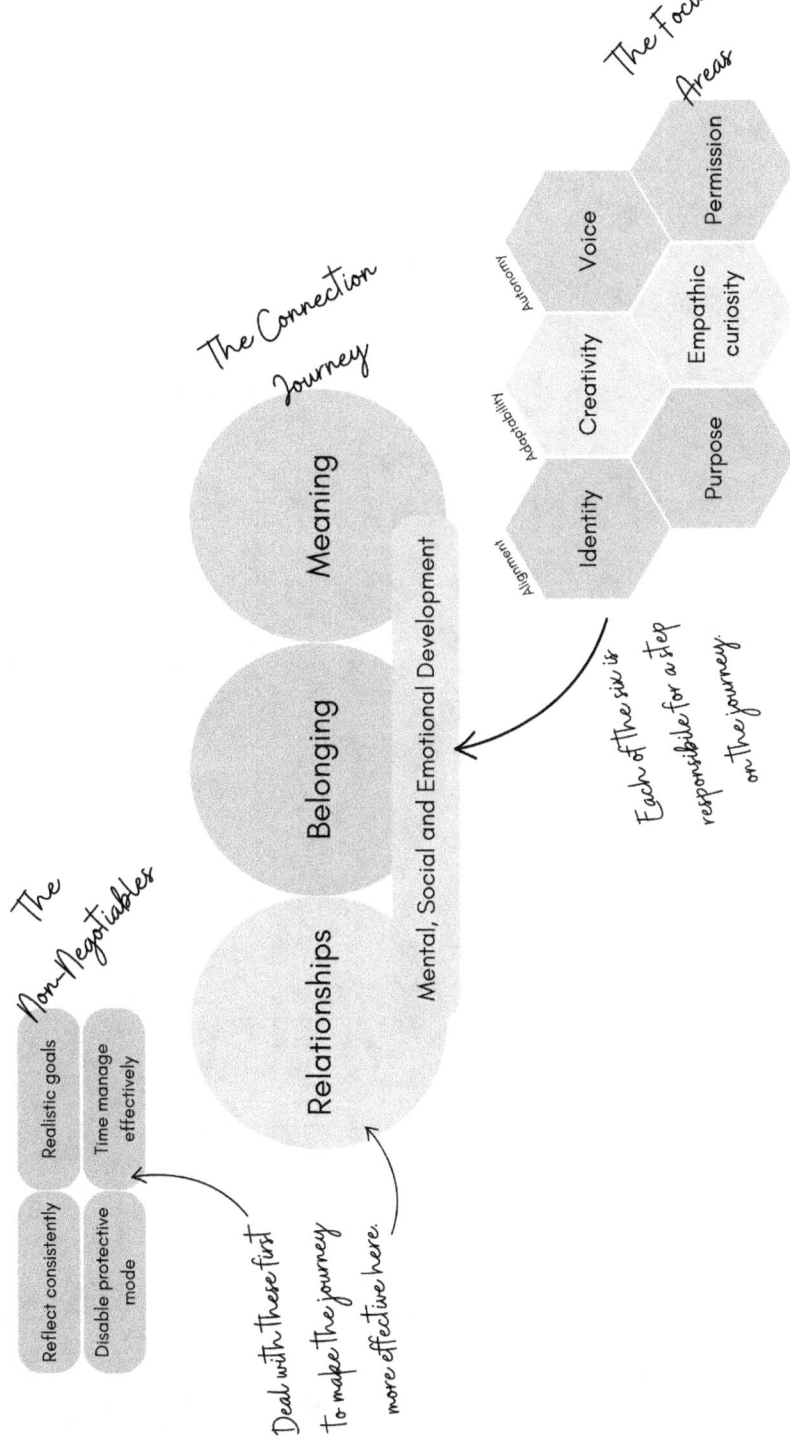

Conclusion 173

References

Abdelzadeh, A., & Lundberg, E. (2017). Solid or flexible? Social Trust from Early Adolescence to Young Adulthood. *Scandinavian Political Studies, 40*(2), 207-227.

Abdulkadiroğlu, A., Pathak, P.A., Schellenberg, J., & Walters, C.R. (2020). Do Parents Value School Effectiveness? *American Economic Review, 110*(5), 1502-1539.

Acharya, P., & Taylor, R. (2012). Innovative Deviance: An Investigation of the Relationships Between Social Control, Creativity and Innovation in Organizations. *Academy of Business Research Journal, 1*, 1-10.

Allen, K.A. (2019). *5 ways to boost students' sense of school belonging*. Monash University Education. www.monash.edu/education/teachspace/articles/5-ways-to-boost-students-sense-of-school-belonging

Allen, K.A. (2020). *The Psychology of Belonging*. Routledge.

Allen, K.A., Gallo Cordoba, B., Ryan, T., Arslan, G., Slaten, C.D., Ferguson, J.K., Bozoglan, B., Abdollahi, A., & Vella-Brodrick, D. (2023). Examining predictors of school belonging using a socio-ecological perspective. *Journal of Child and Family Studies, 32*(9), 2804-2819.

Allen, K.A., Kern, M.L., Rozek, C.S., McInereney, D.M., & Slavich, G.M. (2021). Belonging: A Review of Conceptual Issues, an Integrative Framework, and Directions for Future Research. *Australian Journal of Psychology, 73*(1), 87-102.

Allen, K.A., Kern, M.L., Vella-Brodrick, D., Hattie, J., & Waters, L. (2018). What Schools Need to Know about Fostering School Belonging: A Meta-Analysis. *Educational Psychology Review, 30*, 1-34.

Araújo, U.F.D., Arantes, V.A., Klein, A.M., & Grandino, P.J. (2014). Youth purpose and life goals of students engaged in community and social activities. *Revista Internacional d'Humanitats, 30*, 119-128.

Arslan, G. (2019). School belonging in adolescents: Exploring the associations with school achievement and internalising and externalising problems. *Educational and Child Psychology, 36*(4), 22-33.

Arslan, G. (2021). School belongingness, well-being, and mental health among adolescents: Exploring the role of loneliness. *Australian Journal of Psychology, 73*(1), 70-80.

Australian Curriculum, Assessment and Reporting Authority (ACARA). (2023). *Student Attendance: Key Facts*. www.acara.edu.au/reporting/national-report-on-schooling-in-australia/student-attendance

Australian Institute for Teaching and School Leadership (AITSL). (2023). *ATWD National Trends: Teacher Workforce*. www.aitsl.edu.au/research/australian-teacher-workforce-data/atwdreports/national-trends-teacher-workforce

Australian Institute of Health and Welfare (AIHW). (2021). *Australia's youth: mental illness*. www.aihw.gov.au/reports/children-youth/mental-illness

Bailey, B. (2014). The Impact of Mandated Change on Teachers. In *The Sharp Edge of Educational Change* (pp.112-128). Routledge.

Banwo, B.O., Khalifa, M., & Seashore Louis, K. (2022). Exploring trust: culturally responsive and positive school leadership. *Journal of Educational Administration, 60*(3), 323-339.

Baroutsis, A., Mills, M., McGregor, G., Riele, K., & Hayes, D. (2016). Student voice and the community forum: finding ways of 'being heard' at an alternative school for disenfranchised young people. *British Educational Research Journal, 42*(3), 438-453.

Beghetto, R.A. (2021). There is no creativity without uncertainty: Dubito Ergo Creo. *Journal of Creativity, 31*, 100005.

Beghetto, R.A., & Kaufman, J.C. (2014). Classroom contexts for creativity. *High Ability Studies, 25*(1), 53-69.

Beijaard, D. (2019). Teacher learning as identity learning: models, practices, and topics. *Teachers and Teaching, 25*(1), 1-6.

Bellei, C., Morawietz, L., Valenzuela, J.P., & Vanni, X. (2020). Effective schools 10 years on: factors and processes enabling the sustainability of school effectiveness. *School Effectiveness and School Improvement, 31*(2), 266-288.

Benard, B., & Slade, S. (2009). Moving from Resilience Research to Youth Development Practice and School Connectedness. In Gilman et al. (Ed.), *Handbook of Positive Psychology in Schools* (pp.353-370). Routledge.

Berkovich, I. (2020). Conceptualisations of empathy in K-12 teaching: a review of empirical research. *Educational Review, 72*(5), 547-566.

Biag, M. (2016). A Descriptive Analysis of School Connectedness: The Views of School Personnel. *Urban Education, 51*(1), 32-59.

Bosevska, J., & Kriewaldt, J. (2020). Fostering a whole-school approach to sustainability: learning from one school's journey towards sustainable education. *International Research in Geographical and Environmental Education, 29*(1), 55-73.

Bouchard, K.L., & Berg, D.H. (2017). Students' school belonging: Juxtaposing the perspectives of teachers and students in the late elementary school years (grades 4-8). *The School Community Journal, 27*(1), 107-136.

Brown, B. (2018). *Dare to Lead: Brave Work. Tough Conversations. Whole Hearts.* Random House.

Brown, C., & Shay, M. (2021). From resilience to wellbeing: Identity-building as an alternative framework for schools' role in promoting children's mental health. *Review of Education, 9*(2), 599-634.

Brundtland Commission (formerly the World Commission on Environment and Development). (1987). *Our Common Future.* New York: United Nations General Assembly.

Buheji, M. (2019). *Designing a Curious Life.* AuthorHouse.

Bungay Stanier, M. (2016). *The Coaching Habit: Say Less, Ask More & Change the Way You Lead Forever.* Page Two Books.

Bungay Stanier, M. (2020). *The Advice Trap: Be Humble, Stay Curious & Change the Way You Lead Forever.* Page Two Books.

Burns, A. (2019). *Implementing Whole School Mental Health Approaches: Relationships, reflection and everyday practices* (Doctoral dissertation, University of Manchester).

Burns, E., & Frangiosa, D. (2021). *Going Gradeless, Grades 6-12: Shifting the Focus to Student Learning.* Corwin Press.

Byker, E.J., Putman, S.M., Handler, L., & Polly, D. (2017). Educational Technology and Student Voice: Examining Teacher Candidates' Perceptions. *World Journal on Educational Technology: Current Issues, 9*(3), 119-129.

Cameron, E., & Green, M. (2019). *Making Sense of Change Management: A Complete Guide to the Models, Tools and Techniques of Organizational Change.* Kogan Page Publishers.

Carney, J.V., Kim, H., Hazler, R.J., & Guo, X. (2017). Protective factors for mental health concerns in urban middle school students: The moderating effect of school connectedness. *Professional School Counseling, 21*(1).

Carney, J.V., Kim, I., Bright, D., & Hazler, R.J. (2020). Peer Victimization and Loneliness: The Moderating Role of School Connectedness by Gender. *Journal of School Counseling, 18*(8).

Carton, A.M., & Lucas, B.J. (2018). How can leaders overcome the blurry vision bias? Identifying an antidote to the paradox of vision communication. *Academy of Management Journal, 61*(6), 2106-2129.

Centers for Disease Control and Prevention. (2023). *CDC Healthy Schools: School Connectedness.* www.cdc.gov/healthyschools/school_connectedness.htm

Charteris, J., & Smardon, D. (2019). Democratic contribution or information for reform? Prevailing and emerging discourses of student voice. *Australian Journal of Teacher Education, 44*(6), 1-18.

Collins, J.C., & Porras, J.I. (2005). *Built to Last: Successful Habits of Visionary Companies.* Random House.

Connolly, M., & Kruse, S.D. (2019). Organizational Culture in Schools: A Review of a Widely Misunderstood Concept. *The SAGE Handbook of School Organization,* 177-194.

Cook, K.S., & Santana, J.J. (2020). *Trust: Perspectives in Sociology* (pp.189-204). Routledge.

Cook-Deegan, P. (2016). Seven Ways to Help High Schoolers Find Purpose. *Greater Good Magazine.* https://greatergood.berkeley.edu/article/item/seven_ways_to_help_high_schoolers_find_purpose

Cook-Sather, A. (2018). Tracing the Evolution of Student Voice in Educational Research. *Radical Collegiality Through Student Voice* (pp.17-38). Springer.

Cook-Sather, A. (2020). Student voice across contexts: Fostering student agency in today's schools. *Theory Into Practice, 59*(2), 182-191.

Craig, C.J., Hill-Jackson, V., & Kwok, A. (2023). Teacher Shortages: What Are We Short Of? *Journal of Teacher Education, 74*(3), 209-213.

Crouch, E., Probst, J.C., Radcliff, E., Bennett, K.J., & McKinney, S.H. (2019). Prevalence of adverse childhood experiences (ACEs) among US children. *Child Abuse & Neglect, 92,* 209-218.

Dahlström, H., Oskarsson, M., & Kozina, A. (2023). Using Empathic Curiosity as a Tool for Embracing Diversity. In *European Conference on Educational Research (ECER), Glasgow, August 22-25 2023.*

Daley, S.C. (2019). *School Connectedness and Mental Health in College Students* (Doctoral dissertation, Miami University).

Damon, W., & Malin, H. (2020). The development of purpose: An international perspective. *The Oxford handbook of moral development: An interdisciplinary perspective,* 110.

Damon, W., Menon, J., & Bronk, K.C. (2019). The development of purpose during adolescence. In *Beyond the Self* (pp.119-128). Routledge.

Darling-Hammond, L. (2022). Breaking the Legacy of Teacher Shortages. *Educational Leadership, 80*(2), 14-20.

Day, C., & Gu, Q. (2013). *Resilient Teachers, Resilient Schools: Building and sustaining quality in testing times.* Routledge.

Demanet, J., & Van Houtte, M. (2019). School effects on deviance: an international perspective. *Resisting Education: A Cross-National Study on Systems and School Effects,* 3-26.

Dinçman, M.P. (2021). Mediating Effect of Organizational Identification on the Relationship between Leader-Member Exchange and Organizational Commitment among Primary School Teachers. *Journal of Educational Leadership and Policy Studies, 5*(1).

DiSalvo, D. (2011). *What Makes Your Brain Happy and Why You Should Do the Opposite.* Prometheus Books.

Donaldson, W., & Harter, N. (2019). Leadership in a Constant Liminal Loop: How can i be Authentic when i don't know who i am? *Journal of Leadership Studies, 13*(3), 6-14.

DuPuis, E.M., & Ball, T. (2013). How not what: teaching sustainability as process. Sustainability: Science, *Practice and Policy, 9*(1), 64-75.

El Zaatari, W., & Ibrahim, A. (2021). What promotes adolescents' sense of school belonging? Students and teachers' convergent and divergent views. *Cogent Education, 8*(1).

Erikawati, E. (2023). The Philosophy of Realism in Education. *Journal of Innovation in Teaching and Instructional Media, 4*(1), 70-79.

Evankovich, J. (2022). Implementing Technology to Differentiate Literature Response Questions for Middle School Students. *The Journal of Teacher Action Research, 9*(1).

Fenlon, M.J., & Fitzgerald, B.K. (2021). Creating the future workforce today. Business-Higher Education Forum, Washington, District of Columbia.

Field, J. (2016). *Social capital.* Routledge.

Flak, O. (2019). System of Organizational Terms as a Theoretical Foundation of Cultural Identity Research Using an Online Research Tool for Teaching Reflective Practice. *International Journal of Arts & Sciences, 12*(1), 243-255.

Fleming, D. (2015). Student Voice: An Emerging Discourse in Irish Education Policy. *International Electronic Journal of Elementary Education, 8*(2), 223-242.

Fletcher, T. (2022). *Ten Survival Skills for a World in Flux.* HarperCollins UK.

Ford, J.K., Lauricella, T.K., Van Fossen, J.A., & Riley, S.J. (2021). Creating energy for change: The role of changes in perceived leadership support on commitment to an organizational change initiative. *The Journal of Applied Behavioral Science, 57*(2), 153-173.

Ford, T.G., & Ware, J.K. (2018). Teacher Self-Regulatory Climate: Conceptualizing an Indicator of Leader Support for Teacher Learning and Development. *Leadership and Policy in Schools, 17*(1), 27-51.

Fotheringham, P., Harriott, T., Healy, G., Arenge, G., & Wilson, E. (2022). Pressures and influences on school leaders navigating policy development during the COVID-19 pandemic. *British Educational Research Journal, 48*(2), 201-227.

Fray, L., Jaremus, F., Gore, J., & Harris, J. (2023a). Schooling upheaval during COVID-19: troubling consequences for students' return to school. *The Australian Educational Researcher, 50*(5), 1533-1550.

Fray, L., Jaremus, F., Gore, J., Miller, A., & Harris, J. (2023b). Under pressure and overlooked: the impact of COVID-19 on teachers in NSW public schools. *The Australian Educational Researcher, 50*(3), 701-727.

Fuchsman, K. (2015). Empathy and humanity. *The Journal of Psychohistory, 42*(3).

Fullan, M. (2015). *The New Meaning of Educational Change.* Teachers College Press.

García-Moya, I. (2020). The Concept of Connectedness and Its Relevance to the Study of Student-Teacher Relationships. *The Importance of Connectedness in Student-Teacher Relationships: Insights from the Teacher Connectedness Project*, 27-44.

Ghamrawi, N., Naccache, H., & Shal, T. (2023). Teacher Leadership and Teacher Wellbeing: Any Relationship? *International Journal of Educational Research, 122*.

Gilpin-Jackson, Y. (2013). Practicing in the Grey Area between Dialogic and Diagnostic Organization Development. *Advances in Dialogic OD, 45*(1), 60.

Goddard, A. (2021). Adverse Childhood Experiences and Trauma-Informed Care. *Journal of Pediatric Health Care, 35*(2), 145-155.

Golding, K.S. (2017). *Everyday Parenting with Security and Love: Using PACE to Provide Foundations for Attachment.* Jessica Kingsley Publishers.

Görlich, A., & Katznelson, N. (2015). Educational trust: relational and structural perspectives on young people on the margins of the education system. *Educational Research, 57*(2), 201-215.

Gorny-Wegrzyn, E., & Perry, B. (2021). Inspiring Educators and a Pedagogy of Kindness: A Reflective Essay. *Creative Education, 12*(1), 220-230.

Govender, K., Naicker, S.N., Meyer-Weitz, A., Fanner, J., Naidoo, A., & Penfold, W.L. (2013). Associations between perceptions of school connectedness and adolescent health risk behaviors in South African high school learners. *Journal of School Health, 83*(9), 614-622.

Grant, A. (2021). *Think Again: The Power of Knowing What You Don't Know.* Penguin.

Green, N., & Turner, M. (2017). Creating Children's Spaces, Children Co-Creating Place. *Journal of Childhood Studies, 42*(3), 27-39.

Gregory, J.L. (2017). Trust relationships in schools: supporting or subverting implementation of school-wide initiatives. *School Leadership and Management, 37*(1-2), 141-161.

Gregory, J.L., & Mebane, K.A. (2020). The role of ego threat in professional growth: Fulfilling the ethical intentions of the SEED Model. *Educational Practice and Theory, 42*(1), 5-25.

Griffith, A.N., Larson, R.W., & Johnson, H.E. (2018). How trust grows: Teenagers' accounts of forming trust in youth program staff. *Qualitative Psychology, 5*(3), 340.

Guay, F., Morin, A.J., Litalien, D., Howard, J.L., & Gilbert, W. (2021). Trajectories of self-determined motivation during the secondary school: A growth mixture analysis. *Journal of Educational Psychology, 113*(2), 390.

Gümüş, S., Çağatay Kılınç, A., & Bellibaş, M.S. (2022). The relationship between teacher leadership capacity at school and teacher self-efficacy: the mediating role of teacher professional learning. *School Leadership and Management, 42*(5), 478-497.

Gunter, H., & Thomson, P. (2007). Learning about student voice. *Support for Learning, 22*(4), 181-188.

Hagenauer, G., Reitbauer, E., & Hascher, T. (2013). "It's cool but challenging" The Relevance of Basic Need Fulfillment for Students' School Enjoyment and Emotional Experiences at the Transition from Primary to Secondary Education. *Orbis Scholae, 7*(2), 23-42.

Halliday, A.J., Kern, M.L., Garrett, D.K., & Turnbull, D.A. (2019). The student voice in well-being: A case study of participatory action research in positive education. *Educational Action Research, 27*(2), 173-196.

Han, J., Way, N., Yoshikawa, H., & Clarke, C. (2023). Interpersonal Curiosity and its Association With Social and Emotional Skills and Well-Being During Adolescence. *Journal of Adolescent Research*, 07435584231162572.

Hands, C.M. (2014). Youth Perspectives on Community Collaboration in Education: Are Students Innovative Developers, Active Participants, or Passive Observers of Collaborative Activities? *School Community Journal, 24*(1), 69-97.

Harber, C. (2021). School Uniform and Uniformity. *Post-Covid Schooling: Future Alternatives to the Global Normal*, 139-162.

Hardin, R. (2002). *Trust and Trustworthiness*. Russell Sage Foundation.

Hardy, I. (2015). Data, Numbers and Accountability: The Complexity, Nature and Effects of Data Use in Schools. *British Journal of Educational Studies, 63*(4), 467-486.

Hargreaves, A., & Fink, D. (2004). The seven principles of sustainable leadership. *Educational Leadership, 61*(7).

Haslam, S.A., Jetten, J., Maskor, M., Bentley, S., & Steffens, N. (2021a). The Two-Stage Social Identity Model of High-Reliability Organisations. In *Sustainable Minerals Institute High Reliability Organisations Forum Paper*.

Haslam, S.A., Steffens, N.K., Reicher, S.D., & Bentley, S.V. (2021b). Identity leadership in a crisis: A 5R framework for learning from responses to COVID-19. *Social Issues and Policy Review, 15*(1), 35-83.

Haslam, S.A., Steffens, N.K., Peters, K., Boyce, R.A., Mallett, C.J., & Fransen, K. (2017). A social identity approach to leadership development: The 5R program. *Journal of Personnel Psychology*.

Hattie, J. (2023). *Visible Learning: The Sequel: A Synthesis of Over 2,100 Meta-Analyses Relating to Achievement*. Taylor & Francis.

Hay, G.J., Parker, S.K., & Luksyte, A. (2021). Making sense of organisational change failure: An identity lens. *Human relations, 74*(2), 180-207.

Heinsch, M., Agllias, K., Sampson, D., Howard, A., Blakemore, T., & Cootes, H. (2020). Peer connectedness during the transition to secondary school: a collaborative opportunity for education and social work. *The Australian Educational Researcher, 47*, 339-356.

Henriksen, D., Richardson, C., & Shack, K. (2020). Mindfulness and creativity: Implications for thinking and learning. *Thinking skills and creativity, 37*, 100689.

Hillen, J., & Nevins, M.D. (2019). *What Happens Now?* Jaico Publishing House.

Holden, A.C. (2021). Cultural Influence and Teacher Quality: Perceptions of Self-Efficacy and Self-Permission in Panamanian Educators. *The International Journal of Engineering and Science, 10*(3), 1–14.

Holt-Lunstad, J. (2022). Social Connection as a Public Health Issue: The Evidence and a Systemic Framework for Prioritizing the "Social" in Social Determinants of Health. *Annual Review of Public Health, 43*, 193–213.

Hughes, D.A., & Golding, K.S. (2012). *Creating Loving Attachments: Parenting with PACE to Nurture Confidence and Security in the Troubled Child.* Jessica Kingsley Publishers.

Johnston, O., Wildy, H., & Shand, J. (2021). Projecting student voice by constructing grounded theory. *The Australian Educational Researcher, 48*, 543–564.

Jones, M.A., & Bubb, S. (2021). Student voice to improve schools: Perspectives from students, teachers and leaders in 'perfect' conditions. *Improving Schools*, 1365480219901064.

Jones, S.E., Ethier, K.A., Hertz, M., DeGue, S., Le, V.D., Thornton, J., Lim, C., Dittus, P.J., & Geda, S. (2022). Mental Health, Suicidality, and Connectedness Among High School Students During the COVID-19 Pandemic – Adolescent Behaviors and Experiences Survey, United States, January–June 2021. *MMWR supplements, 71*(3), 16.

Kaptan, O., Korumaz, M., & Uçar, İ. (2022). What do schools sell? The neoliberal transformation of public schools' institutional identities. *The Journal of Academic Social Science Studies, 15*(90).

Keddie, A. (2015). Student voice and teacher accountability: possibilities and problematics. Pedagogy, *Culture & Society, 23*(2), 225–244.

Keren, A. (2020). Trust and Belief. *The Routledge Handbook of Trust and Philosophy*, 109–120.

Kim, H., Carney, J.V., & Hazler, R.J. (2023). Promoting school connectedness: A critical review of definitions and theoretical models for school-based interventions. Preventing School Failure: *Alternative Education for Children and Youth, 67*(4), 256–264.

Korpershoek, H., Canrinus, E.T., Fokkens-Bruinsma, M., & de Boer, H. (2020). The relationships between school belonging and students' motivational, social-emotional, behavioural, and academic outcomes in secondary education: a meta-analytic review. *Research Papers in Education, 35*(6), 641–680.

Kotter, J. (2012). *The 8-Step Process for Leading Change.* Kotter International.

Kotter, J.P., Akhtar, V., & Gupta, G. (2021). *Change: How Organizations Achieve Hard-to-Imagine Results in Uncertain and Volatile Times.* John Wiley & Sons.

Krannich, M. (2019). Antecedents and Effects of Boredom at School: A Matter of Being Over- or Underchallenged.

Lac, V.T., & Cumings Mansfield, K. (2018). What do students have to do with educational leadership? Making a case for centering student voice. *Journal of Research on Leadership Education, 13*(1), 38–58.

Lane, R. (2017). *Peirce on Realism and Idealism.* Cambridge University Press.

Lansford, J.E., Dodge, K.A., Pettit, G.S., & Bates, J.E. (2016). A public health perspective on school dropout and adult outcomes: A prospective study of risk and protective factors from age 5 to 27 years. *Journal of Adolescent Health, 58*(6), 652–658.

Lassig, C. (2021). Creativity talent development: Fostering creativity in schools. *Handbook of Giftedness and Talent Development in the Asia-Pacific*, 1045–1069.

Lejeune, C., & Vas, A. (2014). Institutional Pressure as a Trigger for Organizational Identity Change. *The Institutional Development of Business Schools*, 95.

Long, T., & Guo, J. (2023). Moving beyond Inclusion to Belonging. *International Journal of Environmental Research and Public Health, 20*(20), 6907.

Lubelfeld, M., Polyak, N., & Caposey, P.J. (2018). *Student Voice: From Invisible to Invaluable.* Rowman & Littlefield.

Lundy, L. (2007). 'Voice' is Not Enough: Conceptualising Article 12 of the United Nations Convention on the Rights of the Child. *British Educational Research Journal, 33*(6), 927–942.

Madigan, D.J., & Kim, L.E. (2021). Towards an understanding of teacher attrition: A meta-analysis of burnout, job satisfaction, and teachers' intentions to quit. *Teaching and Teacher Education, 105*, 103425.

Magrì, E. (2020). Empathy, Respect, and Vulnerability. In *The Value of Empathy* (pp.224–243). Routledge.

Mahmoud, Z. (2022). The teachers' perception of the factors that promote the cultivation of creative thinking. Interdisciplinary Research in Counseling, *Ethics and Philosophy, 2*(6), 64–98.

Malin, H. (2018). *Teaching for Purpose: Preparing Students for Lives of Meaning*. Harvard Education Press.

Malin, H., Liauw, I., & Remington, K. (2019). Early Adolescent Purpose Development and Perceived Supports for Purpose at School. *Journal of Character Education, 15*(2), 1–20.

Manwani, K.G., & Gupta, M. (2020). The neuroscience aspects of adolescent behaviour and its implications. *Psychology and Education Journal, 57*(9), 6489–6493.

Marsh, V.L., Lammers, J.C., & Conroy, E. (2021). Students as Changemakers: Five Steps to Advocacy Research. *English Journal, 111*(2), 56–63.

Mayger, L.K., & Hochbein, C.D. (2021). Growing Connected: Relational Trust and Social Capital in Community Schools. *Journal of Education for Students Placed at Risk (JESPAR), 26*(3), 210–235.

Mayseless, O., & Kizel, A. (2022). Preparing youth for participatory civil society: A call for spiritual, communal, and pluralistic humanism in education with a focus on community of philosophical inquiry. *International Journal of Educational Research, 115*(3), 102015.

McDonald, B., Lester, K.J., & Michelson, D. (2023). 'She didn't know how to go back': School attendance problems in the context of the COVID-19 pandemic – A multiple stakeholder qualitative study with parents and professionals. *British Journal of Educational Psychology, 93*(1), 386–401.

Milner IV, H.R. (2014). Culturally Relevant, Purpose-Driven Learning & Teaching in a Middle School Social Studies Classroom. *Multicultural Education, 21*(2), 9–17.

Mitra, D. (2018). Student voice in secondary schools: The possibility for deeper change. *Journal of Education Administration*.

Morton, B.M. (2022). Trauma-Informed School Practices: Creating Positive Classroom Culture. *Middle School Journal, 53*(4), 20–27.

Nadelson, L.S., Nadelson, S.G., Broyles, A., Edgar, J., Einhorn, J., Hatchett, A., Scroggins, T., Skipper, A., & Ulrich, C. (2019). Beyond the Books: Teacher Practices and Perceptions of Teaching Caring and Curiosity. *Journal of Curriculum and Teaching, 8*(3), 84–101.

Nazir, C., & Lin, M. (2023). Beyond empathy: how curiosity promotes to greater care.

Nguyen, C.D., Huynh, T.N., & Tran, N.H. (2022). Overcoming contextual constraints: implementing classroom pedagogical innovation through teacher leadership. *International Journal of Leadership in Education*, 1–19.

Nguyen, T.D., Pham, L.D., Crouch, M., & Springer, M.G. (2020). The correlates of teacher turnover: An updated and expanded meta-analysis of the literature. *Educational Research Review, 31*(3), 100355.

Okabe-Miyamoto, K., Folk, D., Lyubomirsky, S., & Dunn, E.W. (2021). Changes in social connection during COVID-19 social distancing: It's not (household) size that matters, it's who you're with. *PloS One, 16*(1), e0245009.

Orridge, M. (2017). *Change Leadership: Developing a Change-Adept Organization*. Routledge.

Pandya, A., & Lodha, P. (2021). Social Connectedness, Excessive Screen Time During COVID-19 and Mental Health: *A Review of Current Evidence. Frontiers in Human Dynamics, 3*, 45.

Pate, C.M., Glymph, A., Joiner, T., & Bhagwandeen, R. (2023). Students as Co-creators of Educational Environments. In *Handbook of School Mental Health: Innovations in Science and Practice* (pp.187–200). Cham: Springer International Publishing.

Pearce, T.C., & Wood, B.E. (2019). Education for transformation: an evaluative framework to guide student voice work in schools. *Critical Studies in Education, 60*(1), 113–130.

Peng, A., Patterson, M.M., & Joo, S. (2023). What Fosters School Connectedness? The Roles of Classroom Interactions and Parental Support. *Journal of Youth and Adolescence*, 1–12.

Pink, D.H. (2011). *Drive: The Surprising Truth About What Motivates Us.* Penguin.

Pitsakis, K., Biniari, M.G., & Kuin, T. (2012). Resisting change: Organizational decoupling through an identity construction perspective. *Journal of Organizational Change Management, 25*(6), 835–852.

Qvortrup, A., & Lykkegaard, E. (2024). Building back better: lessons learned from a year with COVID-19 caused changes to school and teaching. *Education 3-13, 52*(1), 92–110.

Ralph, T. (2021). Non-compliance as a substitute for voice. *Research Papers in Education, 36*(2), 176–195.

Ramalu, S.S., Nadarajah, G., & Aremu, A.Y. (2020). Turning Students from Job Seekers into Job Creators: The Role of High Impact Entrepreneurship Educational Practices. *International Journal of Innovation, Creativity and Change, 13*(4), 347–372.

Rashad, K. (2018). *Teacher Perceptions of Trust: Principal Behaviors and School Practices* (Doctoral dissertation, Azusa Pacific University).

Ratner, K., Burrow, A.L., Burd, K.A., & Hill, P.L. (2021). On the conflation of purpose and meaning in life: A qualitative study of high school and college student conceptions. *Applied Developmental Science, 25*(4), 364–384.

Ravasi, D., & Canato, A. (2013). How do I know who you think you are? A review of research methods on organizational identity. *International Journal of Management Reviews, 15*(2), 185–204.

Remon, H.C., Taylor, P., & Kuss, A. (2023). Leading a critical transformation: Integrating top-down with bottom-up in an infrastructure approach to school improvement. *Australian Educational Leader, 45*(3), 42–46.

Riley, K. (2019). Agency and belonging: What transformative actions can schools take to help create a sense of place and belonging? *Educational and Child Psychology, 36*(4), 91–103.

Rimm-Kaufman, S., & Sandilos, L. (2015). *Improving Students' Relationships with Teachers to Provide Essential Supports for Learning: Applications of Psychological Science to Teaching and Learning modules.* www.apa.org/education-career/k12/relationships

Robinson, C., & Taylor, C. (2013). Student voice as a contested practice: Power and participation in two student voice projects. *Improving Schools, 16*(1), 32–46.

Robinson, K., & Aronica, L. (2016). *Creative Schools: The Grassroots Revolution That's Transforming Education.* Penguin.

Rolfe, G., Freshwater, D., & Jasper, M. (2001). *Critical Reflection for Nursing and the Helping Professions: A User's Guide.* Palgrave Macmillan.

Rose, I.D., Lesesne, C.A., Sun, J., Johns, M.M., Zhang, X., & Hertz, M. (2022). The relationship of school connectedness to adolescents' engagement in co-occurring health risks: a meta-analytic review. *The Journal of School Nursing*, 10598405221096802.

Rui, Y., & Liu, T. (2023). The effect of online English learners' perceived teacher support on self-regulation mediated by their self-efficacy. *Porta Linguarum Revista Interuniversitaria de Didáctica de las Lenguas Extranjeras*, (40), 215–233.

Ruiz, L.D., McMahon, S.D., & Jason, L.A. (2018). The Role of Neighborhood Context and School Climate in School-Level Academic Achievement. *American Journal of Community Psychology, 61*(3–4), 296–309.

Ryan, R.M., & Deci, E.L. (2022). Self-Determination Theory. In *Encyclopedia of Quality of Life and Well-Being Research* (pp.1–7). Cham: Springer International Publishing.

Ryder, M., & Downs, C. (2022). Rethinking reflective practice: John Boyd's OODA loop as an alternative to Kolb. *The International Journal of Management Education, 20*(3), 100703.

Sahlberg, P. (2020). Will the pandemic change schools? *Journal of Professional Capital and Community, 5*(3/4), 359-365.

Sahlberg, P., & Doyle, W. (2019). *Let the Children Play: How More Play Will Save Our Schools and Help Children Thrive.* Oxford University Press, USA.

Schneider, J. (2017). *Beyond Test Scores: A Better Way to Measure School Quality.* Harvard University Press.

Scott, K. (2017). *Radical Candor: How to Get What You Want by Saying What You Mean.* Pan MacMillan UK.

Šeboková, G., Uhláriková, J., & Halamová, M. (2018). Cognitive and social sources of adolescent well-being: Mediating role of school belonging. *Studia Psychologica, 60*(1), 16-29.

Sethi, J., & Scales, P.C. (2020). Developmental Relationships and School Success: How Teachers, Parents, and Friends Affect Educational Outcomes and What Actions Students Say Matter Most. *Contemporary Educational Psychology, 63*(2), 101904.

Shaheen, F., Khan, H.M.A., & Sindher, R.H.K. (2022). Classroom Processes and Students' Learning. *Pakistan Journal of Humanities & Social Sciences, 10*(2), 822-829.

Shier, H. (2019). Student voice and children's rights: power, empowerment, and "protagonismo". In Peters, M.A. (Ed.). *Encyclopedia of Teacher Education.* Springer Nature Singapore.

Sinek, S. (2019). *The Infinite Game.* Penguin.

Singh, S., Roy, D., Sinha, K., Parveen, S., Sharma, G., & Joshi, G. (2020). Impact of COVID-19 and lockdown on mental health of children and adolescents: A narrative review with recommendations. *Psychiatry Research, 293,* 113429.

Singhal, A., & Svenkerud, P.J. (2019). Flipping the Diffusion of Innovations Paradigm: Embracing the Positive Deviance Approach to Social Change. *Asia Pacific Media Educator, 29*(2), 151-163.

Skaalvik, E.M., & Skaalvik, S. (2021). Collective teacher culture: exploring an elusive construct and its relations with teacher autonomy, belonging, and job satisfaction. *Social Psychology of Education, 24,* 1389-1406.

Spernes, K. (2022). The transition between primary and secondary school: a thematic review emphasising social and emotional issues. *Research Papers in Education, 37*(3), 303-320.

Stacey, M., Wilson, R., & McGrath-Champ, S. (2022). Triage in Teaching: The Nature and Impact of Workload in Schools. *Asia Pacific Journal of Education, 42*(4), 772-785.

Stahl, G., & McDonald, S. (2021). Thinking with habitus in the study of learner identities. *The Handbook of Critical Theoretical Research Methods in Education,* 199-211.

Steger, M.F., O'Donnell, M.B., & Morse, J.L. (2021). Helping students find their way to meaning: Meaning and purpose in education. In *The Palgrave Handbook of Positive Education* (pp.551-579). Cham: Springer International Publishing.

Stern, J. (2018). *A philosophy of schooling: Care and Curiosity in Community.* Springer.

Stirling, S., & Emery, H. (2016). *A whole school framework for emotional well-being and mental health.* London: National Children's Bureau.

Stoll, L. (2020). Creating capacity for learning: Are we there yet? *Journal of Educational Change, 21*(3), 421-430.

Stone, B.A. (2020). Curriculum-centered barriers to child-centered practice and frames for Resistance. *Professing Education, 18,* 51-64.

Strier, M., & Katz, H. (2016). Trust and parents' involvement in schools of choice. *Educational Management Administration & Leadership, 44*(3), 363-379.

Suddaby, R., & Foster, W.M. (2017). History and Organizational Change. *Journal of Management, 43*(1), 19-38.

Summers, J.J., & Falco, L.D. (2020). The development and validation of a new measure of adolescent purpose. *The Journal of Experimental Education, 88*(1), 47–71.

Sun, J., Zhang, R., & Forsyth, P.B. (2023). The Effects of Teacher Trust on Student Learning and the Malleability of Teacher Trust to School Leadership: A 35-Year Meta-Analysis. *Educational Administration Quarterly, 59*(4), 744–810.

Tan, C. (2006). Philosophical perspectives on education. In *Critical Perspectives on Education: An Introduction*, Tan, C., Wong, B., Chua, J.S.M., & Kang, T. (Eds.) (pp.21–40). Prentice Hall.

Tan, S. (2023). Exploiting Disruptive Innovation in Learning and Teaching. In *Learning Intelligence: Innovative and Digital Transformative Learning Strategies: Cultural and Social Engineering Perspectives*, Rajaram, K. (pp.149–176). Singapore: Springer Nature Singapore.

Tataw, D. (2023). Social Capital and Value Creation in Learning Communities: Evidence from a Team-Lecture Hybrid (TLH) Instructional Strategy. *International Journal of Teaching and Learning in Higher Education, 35*(1), 1–19.

Tomkunas, A.J., Welliver, M., Wink, M.N., & LaRusso, M.D. (2023). Should schools "return to normal"? Mixed outcomes resulting from COVID-19 in schools. *Psychology in the Schools, 60*(11), 4618–4636.

Treacy, M., & Leavy, A. (2021). Student voice and its role in creating cognitive dissonance: the neglected narrative in teacher professional development. *Professional Development in Education*, 1–20.

Tschannen-Moran, M. (2014). *Trust Matters: Leadership for Successful Schools*. John Wiley & Sons.

Ungar, M., Russell, P., & Connelly, G. (2014). School-Based Interventions to Enhance the Resilience of Students. *Journal of Educational and Developmental Psychology, 4*(1), 66.

Uslu, F., & Gizir, S. (2017). School belonging of adolescents: The role of teacher-student relationships, peer relationships and family involvement. *Educational Sciences: Theory & Practice, 17*(1), 63–82.

Van Bergen, P., Graham, L.J., & Sweller, N. (2020). Memories of positive and negative student-teacher relationships in students with and without disruptive behavior. *School Psychology Review, 1*(17).

Van Cuylenburg, H. (2021). *Let Go: It's time for us to let go of shame, expectation and our addiction to social media, from The Resilience Project*. Penguin.

Van Orden, K.A., Bower, E., Lutz, J., Silva, C., Gallegos, A.M., Podgorski, C.A., Santos, E.J., & Conwell, Y. (2021). Strategies to Promote Social Connections Among Older Adults During "Social Distancing" Restrictions. *The American Journal of Geriatric Psychiatry, 29*(8), 816–827.

Vaughn, M. (2021). *Student Agency in the Classroom: Honoring Student Voice in the Curriculum*. Teachers College Press.

Verster, M.C., Mentz, E., & du Toit-Brits, C. (2018). A Theoretical Perspective on the Requirements of the 21st Century for Teachers' Curriculum as Praxis. *Literacy Information and Computer Education Journal, 9*(1), 2825.

Virtanen, T.E., Vasalampi, K., Torppa, M., Lerkkanen, M.K., & Nurmi, J.E. (2019). Changes in students' psychological well-being during transition from primary school to lower secondary school: A person-centered approach. *Learning and Individual Differences, 69*, 138–149.

Wagner, T., Kegan, R., Lahey, L.L., Lemons, R.W., Garnier, J., Helsing, D., Howell, A., & Rasmussen, H.T. (2012). *Change Leadership: A Practical Guide to Transforming Our Schools*. John Wiley & Sons.

Walters, A.S. (2023). School absenteeism in the post-pandemic world. *The Brown University Child and Adolescent Behavior Letter, 39*(1), 8–8.

Wang, F., Pollock, K., & Hauseman, C. (2023). Time Demands and Emotionally Draining Situations Amid Work Intensification of School Principals. *Educational Administration Quarterly, 59*(1), 112–142.

Waters, S., Lester, L., Wenden, L., & Cross, D. (2012). A theoretically grounded exploration of the social and emotional outcomes of transition to secondary school. *Australian Journal of Guidance and Counselling, 22*(2), 190–205.

Weger, K., Matsuyama, L., Zimmermann, R., Mesmer, B., Van Bossuyt, D., Semmens, R., & Eaton, C. (2023). Insight into User Acceptance and Adoption of Autonomous Systems in Mission Critical Environments. *International Journal of Human–Computer Interaction, 39*(7), 1423–1437.

Weiss, J.K. (2018). Involving the stakeholders that matter most: Student voice in school reform. *Journal of Ethical Educational Leadership, 1*, 199–208.

Whitehead, J., Schonert-Reichl, K.A., Oberle, E., & Boyd, L. (2023). What do teachers do to show they care? Learning from the voices of early adolescents. *Journal of Adolescent Research, 38*(4), 726–760.

Winton, B.G., Whittington, J.L., & Meskelis, S. (2022). Authentic leadership: making meaning and building engagement. *European Business Review, 34*(5), 689–705.

Wood, R. (2020). Investigating the enhancement of students' engagement with learning activities through the lens of Self-Determination Theory. *European Journal of Teaching and Education, 2*(2), 152–182.

Woods-Groves, S., Choi, T., Bruhn, A.L., & Fernando, J. (2019). Examining teachers' perceptions of K-11 students' 21st century skills and student performance. *Psychology in the Schools, 56*(9), 1434–1454.

Yan, M. (2023). School Refusal: Conceptualization, Leading Factors, and Intervention. *Journal of Education, Humanities and Social Sciences, 8*, 627–633.

You, J., Kim, J., & Lim, D.H. (2021). Organizational learning and change: Strategic interventions to deal with resistance. In *Research Anthology on Digital Transformation, Organizational Change, and the Impact of Remote Work* (pp.723–741). IGI Global.

Yuen, C.Y. (2022). *Multiculturalism, Educational Inclusion, and Connectedness: Well-being, Ethnicity, and Identity among Chinese, South, and Southeast Asian Students*. Routledge.

Zeinalipour, H. (2022). School Connectedness, Academic Self-Efficacy, and Academic Performance: Mediating Role of Hope. *Psychological Reports, 125*(4), 2052–2068.

Zhang, M.X., Mou, N.L., Tong, K.K., & Wu, A.M. (2018). Investigation of the Effects of Purpose in Life, Grit, Gratitude, and School Belonging on Mental Distress among Chinese Emerging Adults. *International Journal of Environmental Research and Public Health, 15*(10), 2147.

Zurn, P., & Shankar, A. (Eds.). (2020). *Curiosity Studies: A New Ecology of Knowledge*. University of Minnesota Press.

www.ingramcontent.com/pod-product-compliance
Lightning Source LLC
Chambersburg PA
CBHW050201130526
44591CB00034B/1673